MAKSIM GORKI

*I am an irreconcilable enemy of
everything low and petty in human desires
and would like everybody with a human face
truly to be a human being.*

MAKSIM GORKI

Modern Literature Monographs

MAKSIM GORKI

Gerhard Habermann

Translated by
Ernestine Schlant

Frederick Ungar Publishing Co.
New York

Translated from the original German and published by
arrangement with Colloquium Verlag, Berlin

891.73
Hllm
89868
Sept 1974

Contents

1

Childhood

In the birth registry of the Church of the Martyr Varvara in Nishni-Novgorod, the birth of Aleksei Maksimovich Peshkov (known as Maksim Gorki) is entered in these words:

Born in 1868, on March 16th, and baptized on the 22nd: Aleksei, son of the lower-middle-class bourgeois Maksim Savvatyevich Peshkov, from the province of Perm, and of his wife Varvara Vassilyevna, both of Orthodox faith. . . .

In 1869, the Peshkov family moved to Astrakhan, where the father was offered a position as wharf supervisor. Aleksei contracted cholera when he was four years old, and his father, who tended him during his illness, also contracted the disease, dying in 1872. *My Childhood,* the first volume of Gorki's autobiographical trilogy, begins with this death. Aleksei's grandmother, Akulina Kashirina, took the boy and his mother back to Nishni. The little boy immediately liked his grandmother, because she seemed happy and had a warm heart. His grandfather, however, was the very opposite. He was tiny and thin, with a big hawk nose, green eyes, and a long red beard. Gorki later wrote:

An extremely strange, crude, colorful life started for me and swept me along with frightful speed. It remains in my memory as a sinister fairy tale. I would now like to discard much of it, but reality is more important than soft emotionalism. Also, I am not talking about myself, but about a way of life—filled with narrow, numb, squalid impressions of the most varied kinds—in which I then grew up and in which to this day [the memoirs were published in 1913] the simple Russian people still vegetate.

In addition to Varvara, the mother of the child, the dyer Kashirin had two sons, and in the sinister, narrow house the depressing atmosphere of all against all reigned supreme. Arguments about the future inheritance, accusations and cursings, bestial brutality, beatings, and outrageous maltreatments were the daily fare. Soon after their arrival, the grandfather beat the boy with switches until he fainted, because of a childish prank.

A period of illness in these surroundings was to prove of great importance for Gorki's later life:

I must have matured rapidly during this time, for I experienced a wealth of new, unique emotions. From that time dates a certain rest-less attentiveness with which I began to observe people, and an extremely subtle sensitivity to all kinds of insults and pain directed at myself or others.

Many beautiful things also appeared in his life, how-ever. The boy made friends with the workers in the dye shop, and most of all he enjoyed listening to his grand-mother and her inexhaustible store of legends, fairy tales, and poems. She remained for him the dearest and most precious person in the world. Her selfless love enriched the boy's inner life and strengthened him for difficult times: "Whenever I think of her, everything evil disappears, the wounds heal, everything becomes different, more attractive, more beautiful, and people seem to be better."

In 1873, Gorki's grandfather divided his estate, the sons started dye shops of their own, and the old man bought a new house with an inn on the ground floor. Aleksei watched with great interest the many tenants and the goings-on in the inn. He saw very little of his mother, because she seldom stayed in the house of her parents. Once in a while she put in an appearance, only to vanish again very quickly. She never developed a good relationship with her son, whom she blamed for her husband's death. The education of the boy was therefore completely controlled by his grandparents. Aleksei was barely six years old when his grandfather taught him Church Slavonic by using the Book of

Psalms and the Book of Hours. Satisfied with the boy's tremendous zest for learning, he even allowed him to play with other children occasionally. Such play, however, was never peaceful, because Aleksei became incensed at the cruelties of the neighbors' children, who took pleasure in getting dogs to fight cocks, in torturing cats, or in making fun of drunken beggars. The games always ended in fights among the children, torn clothes, bloody noses, and resulted in Aleksei's being confined to the house.

Kashirin was in trouble. His sons, who had quickly squandered their inheritance, demanded more money from their father. He therefore secretly lent money at usurious rates until someone reported him to the police. Forced to sell the house, he bought a tenement with an overgrown garden.

One day, after two years, Varvara Vassilyevna reappeared and set herself to teaching her son the ordinary alphabet. In a few days he mastered the intricacies of Cyrillic letters. On the other hand, he found it difficult to learn poems by heart, because he did not understand them. His memory was excellent, however, and he could recall with great accuracy the fairy tales and songs his grandmother taught him. Arithmetic, too, was easy. "I did not like to write, however, and grammar I did not understand at all."

Early in 1876, Aleksei's mother took him to school, but he was not particularly happy about the change. After one month he came home with smallpox, and for a long time he lay all by himself in the attic; only his grandmother took care of him, telling him many tales and finally the story of his parents. Aleksei's father had been born somewhere in Siberia and had run away from home and his father's heavy hand on several occasions. Once, the father had searched after the son

with dogs; another time, he had beaten him so mercilessly that the neighbors had had to interfere and hide
the child from the maniac. His mother died early, and
when Maksim Savvatyevich was nine years of age, his
father died too. The boy was brought up in the house of
his godfather, a cabinetmaker in Perm. One day, the boy
ran away, worked as a guide for blind men around country fairs and finally—then sixteen years old—came to
Nishni, where he found employment in a large wood-
working shop. When he was twenty he was already
known as a skilled carpenter, upholsterer, and interior
decorator. His workshop was next to the houses of the
Kashirins. Vassili Vassilyevich Kashirin had worked
his way up from laboring as a simple barge hauler on
the Volga river to thriving as a rich dye merchant with
four houses and a lot of money, and he even possessed
the uniform of a guildmaster. Aleksei learned how his
parents had met and how many difficulties had had to
be overcome, because the old man Kashirin wanted a
member of the nobility as his son-in-law. The grandmother, however, loved the excellent Maksim Savvatyevich more than her own sons and she helped the two
young lovers.

When Aleksei recovered, he was told that his mother intended to marry the student Yevgeni Vassilyevich
Maksimov from the land-surveying institute. From the
beginning the boy felt a profound antipathy toward his
future stepfather and his mother. Nothing helped to
change the situation, not even promises for presents or
to be allowed, later on, to go to high school to become
a doctor or whatever else he would like. Dark premoni-
tions oppressed him; everything seemed "like a series
of steps, leading somewhere into a dark depth, away
from the mother into solitude."

In the garden he had built a little house—his first

independent achievement; here he spent many days and nights, and the romantic enchantment of this time removed all petty anger from his mind: "This was the calmest, most introspective period in my life . . . during that summer a feeling of confidence in my own strength grew in me."

Because of the swindles perpetrated by a nobleman, Aleksei's grandfather lost such an enormous sum in his financial transactions that he went bankrupt. Again, he had no choice but to sell the house. All the furniture was taken over by Tartar junk dealers and Aleksei cried, because he had to leave his beloved garden. The family could afford to rent only two dark, humid rooms in a basement. Soon after, Aleksei's mother appeared with the stepfather. Both looked tired; his mother was pale and thin, and her eyes were burning with fever. The stepfather had gambled all his money away. He had to interrupt his studies in Moscow and accept a position as an office clerk in the suburb of Sormovo. There, Aleksei's parents moved to an apartment in an attic, in a new house with bare, unpapered walls, crowded with cockroaches. The boy lived with his grandmother in the kitchen, because she too was without a home. In a fit of rage, his grandfather had thrown her out once more.

Early in the mornings, when the sirens of the factory called people to work, Aleksei would stand on a bench and look through the windowpane across the roofs; he often saw lanterns at the gate of the plant, which was wide open "like the toothless, black mouth of an old beggar—absorbing a shuffling crowd." At noon the howling of the sirens was heard again. The gates opened and "the dark mouth spit the masses out again." Hardly ever could Aleksei see the blue sky, because day after day thick smoke hung like a flat gray ceiling over the roofs and the sooted snow: "It paralyzed the imagination, and the eye tired because of its desperate, monotonous color."

The rooms always smelled of smoke. Aleksei's grandmother worked hard from daybreak until late at night and went to bed tired; his mother was expecting a child, coughed a great deal, and stared by the hour at the bare walls or the dirty streets. Never did the boy hear a kind word from her. All she offered were commands: "Come here, hand me this, fetch that. . . ." She often hit him with a leather strap because he had played in the streets with other children. The stepfather too was very severe with him. Frequently he fought with his wife; then Aleksei was locked up in the kitchen. The boy was overcome with a feeling of deep desperation, "the awareness of loneliness in a gray, lifeless, and grotesque world."

Yevgeni Vassilyevich was dismissed from his job for shady dealings with the workers' ration cards. Soon he found new employment as cashier for the railroads, and the family moved into the basement of a large stone house. His mother immediately took Aleksei back to school. He wore shoes, a coat made from an old jacket of his grandmother, a yellow shirt and pants "to grow into." Each piece of his wardrobe would have sufficed to make him the laughingstock of his classmates, and because of his yellow shirt he was called "ace of diamonds." He soon coped with the boys; he won over the teacher and the priest, however, only after considerable time and through his studious zeal.

One day the child saw his stepfather strike his mother, who was kneeling on the floor, with the tip of his boots driven into her chest. In blind rage, the boy stabbed his stepfather with the bread knife. His mother pulled him away. Never could Maksim Gorki forget this terrible scene. For him, these were

. . . the horrors of uncivilized Russian life, which weigh you down like lead and represent living, sad reality; a reality that in all its brutality is valid to this day and that one has to know down to its roots to be able to tear it radically out of the consciousness and the soul of the people, out of the sordid, humiliating life.

Because the situation between Aleksei and his parents had become unbearable, the boy had to move back with his grandparents. Life was strange in their lodgings in the basement. The grandfather had turned into an absolute miser. He begged old acquaintances for money and then lent it out at usurious rates. To support his grandmother, Aleksei decided to make money on his own. Every Sunday early in the morning he went out to collect bones, rags, and scraps of iron. During the week he pursued this business after school. His weekly income was between thirty and fifty kopecks, sometimes even more. It was still more lucrative to steal wood and boards at the fairgrounds and from the timber yards along the Oka. Many children were organized into gangs, some of whom even assaulted drunken coachmen and artisans in the suburbs. The Peshkov gang, however, stayed away from these thefts.

School was hard during this time. Aleksei's classmates made fun of the "ragman," the "beggar," the "bandit," and finally told the teacher they could no longer sit next to him because he smelled so terribly:

I remember how deeply wounded I was by this accusation and how hard it was for me after this, to continue school. It was malevolent slander. I always washed very carefully and never went to school in the same clothes in which I collected rags.

Finally Aleksei passed the third-grade exam and was rewarded with an edition of the Gospels, a bound volume of Krylov's fables, and an unbound book with the incomprehensible title *Fata Morgana.* He received a special citation for "good progress made in the sciences."

At last he was out of school and could roam with his gang from morning to night.

This free life was not meant to last long, however: "It seemed to be my destiny to be shaken and tossed about." Once again, Aleksei's stepfather had been dismissed from his job, and once again he had disappeared. The boy's mother and the newborn baby had to take shelter at his grandfather's. Because the mother was very weak, Aleksei took care of the baby. In August 1878, Varvara Vassilyevna died of consumption. After the burial, the grandfather said to the boy: "Well, Leksei, you are not a medal that I can hang around my neck—there is no more room here for you, go out among the people."

With the words "... and I went out among strangers," Gorki concluded the memoirs of his childhood.

2

Apprenticeship

In these hard times among strangers, the boy Aleksei found out about the falsity and meanness of people, but also about their greatness and kindness, in a world in which a kind heart is considered stupidity.

Having reached the age of ten, Aleksei became an apprentice in a shoe salon in the main street of the city. From morning to night, he had to clean the apartment and the store, keep the clothes of the boss, his wife, and the two salesmen in good order, chop and carry wood for all the stoves, and help the mistress in the kitchen. It was also his duty to deliver goods. Despite all these activities, he learned nothing in the store, because nobody took the trouble to teach him. Overworked, he still suffered from boredom. With no one to talk to, he observed his surroundings sharply and critically. His boss and the employees spoke only badly of the world, were full of envy and ill will, and found nothing praiseworthy in anyone. Ever more frequently Aleksei wondered how he could have himself chased away. This came about unexpectedly. One day he burned his hands on the gas burner, and his grandmother took him home.

During the summer months, he went with his grandparents into the woods, gathering wood, herbs, berries, mushrooms, and nuts. His grandmother taught him how to distinguish plants. His admiration for her increased daily, and he considered her "the best and wisest of all human beings." Everything they gathered they sold, and they lived on their earnings from these sales. Aleksei felt especially at ease in the woods:

It provided peace for my soul and made me forget all the incongruities and humiliations. At the same time, it heightened my intellectual receptivity, sharpened my eyes and ears, strengthened my memory, and deepened my sensitivity.

In fall of 1879, Aleksei's grandfather apprenticed the boy to a relative, the illustrator Vassya Sergeyev. The two-story house, in which he then went to live, looked like a coffin. It stood next to a ravine that served as a garbage dump. The house was run by Vassya Sergeyev's mother, a loud, ill-tempered woman, who got up every morning at six o'clock and washed in a hurry. Then, dressed only in her underclothes, she knelt in front of the icon and complained to God for a long time and in a very loud voice about her difficult lot, her children, and her daughter-in-law. Aleksei could do nothing right. She was enraged when on occasion the good-natured Vassya tried to teach Aleksei to paint; she poured oil and beer over the designs, tore up the paper, and wiped everything off the table. She and her daughter-in-law considered the eleven-year-old a servant and made life hard for him. In this they had the support of Vassya's brother Victor. This Victor had Aleksei polish his shoes three times a day, and in thanks for this he spit on Aleksei's head. Again the boy had to chop wood, wash dishes, scrub the floors, and do the shopping. He had not one minute for himself in this miserable, deprived life.

The family, however, made certain that Aleksei went to church. Actually, he liked it. Church was the only place where he could be by himself, and there he felt as free as in the woods. He resented, however, the prescribed prayers that he had to learn by heart. When the cruelties of the day oppressed him too much, he began to think up his own stories. On quiet evenings, when the weather was not too cold and snowy, he preferred to wander in the streets and explore the most secret corners: "I was as alone as the moon in the sky; my shadow was my only company and ran silently ahead of me." He sometimes stopped curiously in front of brightly lit windows. As in a magic mirror, he saw people pray, beat each other, play cards, kiss, or be involved in conversations. These scenes remained forever in his memory.

With the arrival of spring, a painful longing came over him "to go some place where people argue less, molest God less with their obtrusive complaints, and judge their neighbors less malignantly." One bright morning he ran away with the twenty kopecks he was supposed to use to buy bread. He lived for a few days on handouts from the good-natured cargo haulers at the wharf, and he spent the nights at the docks. One of these people found him a job as a dishwasher on the steamboat *Dobry*—for two rubles a month. The ship traveled the route between Perm and Nishni and had in its tow a barge where prisoners exiled to Siberia stood in an iron cage on the deck. From six in the morning until midnight a lot of dishes had to be washed.

Aleksei's immediate boss was the chief cook Smury, a giant with a swollen copper-red nose, bushels of hair on his hands and in his ears, and an enormous moustache. A long time ago, he had been a master sergeant, and when he spoke, he seemed to be barking. Most unusual was the library that he carried in a black, steel-framed suitcase: next to Nekrasov were *Omir's Instructions*; next to memoirs on artillery a book on the eradication of bugs. Other items included the newspaper *Iskra* from 1864, legends of saints, books by Dumas *père,* Gogol, and others. While Smury rested in his hammock, Aleksei had to read to him.

The cook was a philosopher of a kind and believed that in order to become smart one had to read the "right books." He said to Aleksei: "Always read hard—if you don't understand a book, read it seven times, and if you still don't understand, read it twelve times." Although they rarely had the same taste, Smury taught Aleksei to love books and thus became the first teacher of the future writer. The two became so accustomed to each other that Smury often released him from his work, so that Aleksei could read to him. This, of course, made those who had to do Aleksei's dishes very jealous. They tried in many ways to harm the "bookworm," as they called him.

One day, one of them accused Aleksei of stealing. Although the boy was innocent and Smury stood up for him, he was dismissed upon arrival in Nishni and paid eight rubles—the first major sum of money that he had ever earned. Smury, on taking leave of Aleksei, kissed him on the cheek and said, "My boy, this is not the place for you. You ought to learn something. Keep your eyes open and your mouth closed—and read, you hear me? Books are a man's best friends." As a farewell present he gave the boy a pearl-embossed tobacco pouch: "Deep sorrow came over me. I almost cried when I saw him walking back to the steamer, alone, heavy, imposing."

Aleksei had no choice but to return to his grandparents. They had, in the meantime, moved to a little clay hut. His grandmother consoled the boy, who took it very badly that he had been chased off the boat as a thief. She counseled young Aleksei: "Keep all the good in your mind and forget all the evil."

To make some money, the boy caught birds. Day after day the twelve-year-old sat in a ravine, hidden behind bushes. He felt sorry for the happy birds and would have much preferred to watch them and listen to them, but to sell them meant financial independence.

With the first snow of 1880, the grandfather took Aleksei back to Sergeyev, the illustrator. Little had changed there. In the evenings, however, the family

called on the boy to tell them of his trips. Aleksei enjoyed
reminiscing about the colorful and interesting life
on the boat and in the woods. He forgot his dull listen-
ers and involved himself completely in his narrations.
The women had never been on a boat. When he talked
about Smury and his books, they looked at him sus-
piciously. The old woman thought that all books were
written by imbeciles and heretics, and the young woman
considered reading a dangerous activity, particularly
among young people.

Despite such opposition Aleksei spent every free
minute reading: "Sadness and laughter come over me
when I think back to how many humiliations and trou-
bles I owed to my recently kindled rage to read." When
the family went to evening services, he rushed to the
attic, where he had hidden the thick novels lent him by
a tailor's wife from next door. When the Sergeyevs suddenly rang the doorbell, he ran madly around the kitch-
en, "in order to eliminate any traces of the crime." He
hid the book in the vent of the stove and tried, without
success, to clean the lamp, which was smeared with drip-
pings. The old woman saw immediately that the wick
had burned down, and she prophesied a bad end for the
boy. Finally, when they had all gone to sleep, the old
woman on the stove, he took out the book again and
went to the window, to continue reading in the moon-
light.

Sometimes he took the shining copper casserole
from the wall, hoping to generate more light with it.
Whenever the night was too dark, he climbed on the
bench below the icon and read there, standing, by the
shimmer of the eternal light, until he fell on the bench,
overcome with exhaustion, the book still in his hands.
Whenever the old woman discovered him, she started to
scream and hit him with the book.

Aleksei had great difficulty in hiding the heavy volumes he borrowed from the tailor's wife. He therefore began to borrow small, trashy novels from a store, where he had to pay a kopeck for each. He did not enjoy these books, however, "because with high-sounding words they related totally unlikely things." Best of all he liked historical novels and legends of the saints. While he became more and more of an expert in finding hiding-places and time to read, his debts at the store increased. When they amounted to forty-seven kopecks, the store-owner threatened to debit the account of the Sergeyevs. Aleksei's salary went to his grandfather and he received nothing. He thought for a long time and finally decided to steal the money. That, however, was not simple. After tormenting himself for three days he told his master. Sergeyev thought hard and then said, "You see where reading gets you. No matter how, books always bring you misfortune." Then he gave Aleksei half a ruble and promised to subscribe for the new year to a good periodical that the boy could then read.

From that time on, during tea, Aleksei read to the family from the *Moscow Leaflets*. This periodical contained novels by Vashkov and Rokshanin as well as other boring literary products. Aleksei was not especially enthusiastic about reading aloud, because this kept him from understanding the text. His audience, however, greatly enjoyed these sessions and listened with close attention. Because the feuilleton section of the paper did not contain enough material to fill an evening, he was allowed to bring out the volumes his master had illustrated. He was even permitted to read them in the kitchen. The landlady made sure, however, to extinguish the light. Every day then, in secret, he gathered stearin leftovers, put them in a can, covered them with oil that he had taken from the holy lamp, twirled a wick from mending yarn, and then read by the light of this horrible lamp. Although the smoke hurt his eyes, reading recompensed him for all inconveniences:

My relation to books became ever more intimate. I felt as a drunkard feels about brandy—I could no longer live without them. They proved to me that out there, in the world, a kind of life different from the one that surrounded me was pulsating and that people capable of great deeds existed there. No, under no circumstances did I want to remain in my present surroundings.

With each book the difference between Russia and the other countries struck him more deeply than before. Life on the other side of the border seemed easier, more interesting, and better. One day he happened to read Balzac's *Eugenie Grandet,* which he thought beautiful. He had finally found a "real book," as Smury would have called it, which told of "living people," whose very gestures and words spelled truth.

In the spring of 1881, a beautiful, black-eyed young widow had moved with her five-year-old daughter and her mother into the apartment below. The little girl grew up almost without supervision. Aleksei played with her as often as he found time to and told her fairy tales. One evening he met the gracious, exciting widow. For a long time he had secretly called her "Queen Margot" after a Dumas heroine. When she saw how well the children got along, she wanted to present Aleksei a gift. He, however, asked her to lend him books. She gave him Pushkin's poems, which he read immediately. They captivated him in their simplicity and musicality and "for a long time prose seemed unnatural." He visited his Queen Margot every Sunday and talked about the books he had read. She counseled him to read books by Russian authors above all else, so that he would become better acquainted with the life of his own people. He therefore read Akhsakov's *Family Chronicle,* Petsherski's *In the Woods,* Turgenev's *Memoirs of a Hunter,* and many others:

These books cleansed my soul of all the ugly impressions that pitiful reality had deposited in it. They nourished in me the firm conviction that I was not alone and would not perish.

Gorki never forgot his Queen Margot and in many of his writings he built a monument in her honor.

After Pentecost, he left the Sergeyevs and for seven rubles a month washed dishes on the steamer *Perm.* The most interesting person on board proved to be the broad-shouldered stoker Yakov Shumov. He knew wonderful stories and boasted of having seen all the countries of the world. Aleksei had started to write down poems and songs that he liked and impressions that he had experienced either actually or through reading. Later he added his own verses. From all that he had heard and read he fabricated his own world,

. . . which became a protection against bad contacts and the evil poison of life. Totally overworked with senseless activities and arbitrarily humiliated, I nevertheless solemnly promised myself to help people and to serve them loyally once I was grown up.

In this solemn promise of the child may be found the key to the deep love of humanity and the indestructible idealism of the poet. As his later development shows, the sufferings of his youth endowed him with that keen quality of a fighter which to the end of his life made him stand up for humanity, freedom, and justice.

When the boat trips stopped in the late fall of 1881, Aleksei became an apprentice in a shop where icons were painted and sold. Early in the mornings, when everybody was still asleep, he had to get the samovar started for twenty painters, then he cleaned up, together with the apprentice Pavel, mixed egg yolks for the colors,

and went with the salesman at the break of dawn through
still, desolate streets to the Nishni bazaar. In the store
he had ample opportunity to observe people. The buyers
of the icons were usually tight-mouthed farmers. The
bazaar was also the meeting place for theologians and
heretics; there he heard for the first time of the bitter
fights of the followers of the Nikonian Church and of
their persecutions:

The words police, search, jail, trial, Siberia, which one constantly
heard in their talks about the persecutions that they had endured, fell
into my soul like burning coal and stirred my pity for those old men.

Only later did he recognize that the spite of these heretics
was nothing but "the Oriental passivity of people whose
faith was spiritually petrified by the fetters of prejudice
and dogma."

The atmosphere in the shop itself was altogether
different. A haphazard crowd of strong, wild young men
sat crowded around tables in two rooms. They sang mel-
ancholy songs and smoked, while they brushed precisely
marked segments of icons. Aleksei soon discovered that
this piecework, which had nothing in common with art,
satisfied none of them. They all welcomed Aleksei's
stories in the evenings, when he told them about his life
as a dishwasher, or any other stories. The more fantastic
these stories, the more attentively the men listened.
Aleksei dramatized little stories and performed them.
Tremendous applause accompanied his imitations of
merchants and customers at the bazaar.

Years later, Stefan Zweig described Gorki's talents
as an actor, after Zweig had visited him in Sorrento:

While telling a story, he lived it and, living it, he changed into the
character that he was describing, and I understood him through
the mimetic expressions of his face without understanding the
language. . . . Inadvertently, he turned into the person that he

portrayed. I remember how he described an old, tired hunchback, whom he had encountered during his travels. His head sank, his shoulders fell, his eyes—intensely blue and shining when he began the narration—became dark and tired, his voice cracked: without knowing it, he had changed into the old man.

Everybody in the workshop liked Aleksei and called him their "consoler," because they all were unhappy with their dull life, although no one ever attempted to change anything. For Aleksei this was unbearable. He was not made to be a sufferer:

I felt that I was swimming in the same river with all the others, except that for me the water was much colder and did not carry me along as easily, so that at times I thought I was slowly drowning. Would I never find anything better? Was I destined to live forever as all the people around me lived?

In the store, arguments with the salesman increased, and in this disruptive, malcontent frame of mind Gorki decided to go back to work on a steamship "in order to run away to Persia."

He would most certainly have attempted this, if he had not, by sheer accident, run into his former master on the riverbanks of the Oka during Easter week of 1883. Sergeyev persuaded him to work for him as a supervisor for five rubles a month and five kopecks per dinner. Aleksei was very sad when he had to leave the painters, who did not want him to go away.

Aleksei lived in Sergeyev's house for almost two years. The apartment of Queen Margot was occupied by a family with many children. The five daughters and two sons went to the gymnasium and provided him amply with reading materials. Like a starving person, he devoured works by Turgenev, Scott, and Dickens, while Gogol's *Dead Souls,* Dostoevski's *Memoirs from the House of the Dead,* and Tolstoi's *Three Kinds of Death* inspired him with an indefinable aversion.

In the evenings, the young people met in front of the house. They talked about books and poems—subjects about which Aleksei also could talk, having, in fact, read more than they. The brothers and sisters talked about school and their teachers, and Aleksei envied them for being able to study and get an education. At six every morning he had to go to the fairgrounds, where he supervised a rather mixed group of workers. During the winter months, work at the fairgrounds came to a standstill, and he again had to play the role of the servant, as in previous times. This time, however, he had his evenings off.

On Sundays, he liked to go to Millionaya Street, where the barefoot tramps roamed about. He observed these outcasts with great attention. They did not like to work and stole madly; occasionally he saw them loading cargo; in emergencies, such as fires or heavy ice on the river, they worked with great dedication and all their strength. When his boss found out about these walks, he was shocked and would not let Aleksei go there any more; he therefore went secretly. The fifteen-year-old boy felt like "an old man" and found life sinister and stifling. He never drank and did not go after girls: "Instead of these two narcotics, I had books. The more I read, however, the more difficult it was to continue the void and useless life that I thought people led." The most contradictory feelings confused the extremely sensitive boy: on the one hand, he profoundly distrusted the meanness and cruelty of the world and he dreamed of a solitary life with books in a convent or a secluded hut in the woods; on the other hand, he wanted, like the honorable heroes of French novels, to fight the powers of evil and malevolence. While one part of him wanted to be as far away from people as possible, the other part loved them sincerely and wanted to come to the rescue of all sufferers.

He concluded that "I have to do something with myself; otherwise I shall perish."

A student by the name of Nikolai Yevreinov lived in a room in the attic of Sergeyev's house; he and Aleksei had often talked about books. The nineteen-year-old student had a high opinion of Aleksei's intellectual capacities and advised him to go to Kazan, where he could live with Nikolai's mother and, during fall and winter, could go to the gymnasium. All he had to do was to pass "a few exams," and he would be eligible for a scholarship at the university and could be a "professor" within four or five years. This sounded so convincing that finally, in the fall of 1884, Aleksei left for Kazan, full of hopes and accompanied by the blessings of his grandmother.

3

Gorki's "Universities"

In the semi-Tartar city of Kazan, the Yevreinov family (mother and two sons) occupied a small apartment at the end of a shabby narrow street. Behind it lay a burned-out lot, full of ruins overgrown with weeds. Stray dogs lived and died in the cavernous basements of these ruins: "I can still see this basement, because it was destined to be one of my universities."

The tiny, gray-haired widow Yevreinov lived on a small pension and every day had to conjure up all "the tricks of kitchen economics" to serve a hearty meal to three growing young men; she never counted herself. Aleksei had a bad conscience over each piece of bread she gave him—"a strange fellow with uncouth looks and bad manners"—and he therefore went to look for work. As a rule he left the house so as not to be there for the big meal. When the weather was bad, he took refuge in a basement of the ruins: "Surrounded by the smell of dead cats and dogs, the falling rain, and the howling wind, I soon realized that the university had simply been a foolish fantasy."

He pulled himself together and went down to the Volga. At the docks one could easily find a job for fifteen to twenty kopecks a day. In Nishni he had watched the barefoot tramps on Millionaya Street, but he had since become one of them. He lived with them and with cargo haulers and rogues of all kinds.

He later described these types in his works, but without attempting to glorify them. He was not, moreover, the "apostle of the barefoot tramps," as he is still called incorrectly. Gorki liked active people who appreciated life and wanted to enhance it: "The Russian barefoot tramp is a much more horrible phenomenon than I know how to describe, above all in his rigid despair, in his self-negation, and in his self-imposed exile from life." At the time, only the thwarting of his hopes for an education drove him into their company.

Fortunately, he also met other people during that time, such as the cheerful student Guri Pletnyov: "When he found out what difficulties and dangers I had to face, he invited me to move in with him and proposed to make a schoolteacher out of me."

Aleksei left the Yevreinovs and entered a gay and unusual place, the Marusovka. This was a large, dilapidated house, inhabited by hungry students, prostitutes, and various outcasts. Guri lived in the hallway under the staircase. He and Aleksei took turns sleeping on Guri's cot; one slept during the day, the other one at night. Guri worked as night editor at a newspaper and made eleven kopecks a night. Aleksei tortured himself with Russian grammar. To his relief he soon found out that he was too young to apply for a position, even if he should pass the teachers' exam. He could drop the painful study in good conscience.

The colorful inhabitants of the Marusovka provided ample opportunity for Aleksei to watch people. The house was a beehive. From morning to night the crooked hallways buzzed with the clatter of seamstresses and their sewing machines; chorus girls practiced; a half-crazy actor recited in a loud voice; a student sang scales in a deep basso; and drunken prostitutes bawled.

Aleksei made his living by hauling cargo and for a time worked as porter and gardener in the house of Mme. Cornet, a French woman and a general's widow. He recalls this time in detail in his *Reminiscences of Tolstoi.*

Aleksei's most valuable acquaintance was Andrei Derenkov, the owner of a small grocery store. He belonged to the Narodniki party, which held that the farmers and not the workers were the mainstay of the revolution. In order to incite the farmers to fight czarism, the Narodniki went into the villages—among the populace—and for this reason were called the "popularists." From the catastrophe of 1881 on, however, this movement declined considerably.

In his apartment behind the store, Derenkov had a rich library of banned and rare books that were amply used by the students of Kazan's schools and by sympathizers with the revolution. Frequently more than twenty young people met here, worrying about the future of the Russian people. Constantly excited, they were inflamed by newspaper articles and incidents in the city and at the university, and they debated incessantly and hotly. Aleksei had never before had contact with such a revolutionary circle and could hardly follow their arguments. "The truth was dissipated in an avalanche of words, like the fat in the soup of poor people."

At least he understood that they were trying to improve and change life. They, however, haughtily ignored his desire to catch up rapidly with the issues involved and condescendingly called him an "autodidact and son of the populace," which he disliked immensely. The astonished and distrustful Aleksei heard the intelligentsia speak of a people he had never met: for them the people were the embodiment of all wisdom, greatness of soul, of generosity—a godlike, unified being. They also talked a lot about a will to live, imbued with warmth and love of mankind, and of the desire to build a life of freedom, according to new principles. All this sounded wonderful and despite his bitter experiences, Aleksei was finally overcome with enthusiasm. Instead of going to work, he read everything he could find, such as Lavrov's *Historical Letters,* Chernyshevski's *What Is to Be Done?,* essays by Pisarev, *King Hunger,* and Karl Marx's *Das Kapital.* When fall approached, he took a job in Vassili Semyonov's bakery.

As Gorki later confessed, this period was the hardest

time in his life. He described it later in his stories "The Principal," "Konovalov," and "Twenty-six Men and a Girl." Hardest to bear was the effect of his new surroundings on his attitude toward life. He had to work fourteen hours a day in a sticky, smoky basement, and he no longer found time to read Derenkov's books. On holidays he was dead tired; he slept or stayed with his colleagues. Some of them thought him a crazy clown, while others loved him with the naive attachment children have for someone who can tell lovely stories: "Who can remember all the stories I told them! Of course, they were all designed to create hope in the possibility of a different, more purposeful, and easier life."

He imagined with pride that he "enlightened the people" with his propaganda speeches. Often, however, Aleksei felt very frustrated by his lack of knowledge and his inability to answer the simplest questions of everyday life. Whenever he talked about the selfless love of the students who "were seeking the path for the emancipation of the people," they laughed at him mercilessly. He, on the other hand, was incensed at the humble hopelessness with which his colleagues at the bakery submitted to the inhuman brutalities of the drunk Semyonov.

In spring of 1887, Aleksei left the bakery and tried a number of different jobs. He sang for a while as a tenor in the theater chorus. He and Feodor Chaliapin had to audition for the same director, who then sent Chaliapin (who was to become one of the greatest singers of his day) away as "unfit." Aleksei then worked as a helper in a circus. At one time, he wanted to become an acrobat. This was not feasible, because his bones were no longer soft enough. Just at the right moment Derenkov shut down his grocery store and opened a bakery. The profits from this business would go to the revolutionary groups.

Aleksei found employment as a baker. He provided
students with baskets full of rolls under which books
were hidden. The bakery and the store soon did such
good business that Derenkov had to look for larger
premises. Aleksei hoped for a helper in his chores, because he was already "totally numb" with exhaustion.
As a rule he could not sleep more than three to four
hours each night, and during work he could read only
while the dough was rising.

One day, a cousin of Aleksei's wrote that his grandmother had died. She had fallen in front of the church
while begging. She had broken a leg and after a week
gangrene had set in: "I did not cry when I heard of her
death; I only remember that I shuddered as in an icy
wind." How much he would have loved to tell someone
about his grandmother, how kind and wise she had been,
and how motherly toward all human beings! No one
would have listened to him, however, and this hurt him
very much. In his memoirs Gorki reflects briefly: "It had
therefore to remain untold and had to be overcome."

Because Aleksei was less and less satisfied with the
student circle, he searched constantly for new acquaintances. He went to see the workers in the factories and
frequently visited the Spaski convent, where he talked
with the novices and the monks and sometimes even
helped them with their baking. From time to time, he
also went back to Semyonov's bakery, where his old
colleagues gave him warm welcomes. In his novel *A
Confession,* Gorki later testified to the experiences of
that time, when strange people must have interested him.

In December 1887, student riots erupted in Kazan,
and many of his acquaintances were put in jail. Their
leader, incidentally, was Lenin, then Vladimir Ulyanov,
who was subsequently expelled from the university.
Aleksei did not understand the motives of this rebellion.

He saw only the contradictions between the words, actions, and feelings of people: "Life unrolled like an endless chain of animosities and cruelties—like an uninterrupted despicable fight over the possession of irrelevancies."

The nineteen-year-old boy could not find a foothold anywhere and tormented himself repeatedly with the feeling of uselessness and alienation. It appeared to him that his work and even his life had lost all meaning. On December 12 he bought a pistol loaded with four bullets and shot himself in the chest. The bullet pierced his lung. Although his condition at first seemed hopeless, he recovered quickly from an operation. After ten days he was released from the hospital: "One month later I was back at work in the bakery. I was ashamed of myself and felt utterly foolish."

Gorki gave the reasons for this attempted suicide in his story "An Incident in the Life of Makar." In his memoirs, however, he comments: "I did not succeed too well. The narration is clumsy, unsatisfactory, and lacks inner truth."

By the end of March 1888, the Narodnik revolutionary Mikhail Romas suggested that Aleksei go with him to his village Krasnovidovo on the Volga. He owned a grocery store there and needed help.

At first, this meant a nicer life for Aleksei. Romas spent much time with him and succeeded above all in making the young man lose his feeling of inferiority. Lots of good books were available in the house, almost exclusively scientific works by Taylor, Spencer, Darwin, Dobrolyubov, Goncharov, and others. Here Aleksei first read Hobbes' *Leviathan* and Machiavelli's *The Prince.*

Romas had been imprisoned for two years for his revolutionary activities and had subsequently been exiled for ten years to the region around Yakutsk, where he met the student Vladimir Korolenko, who had since become known as a writer. Neither Aleksei nor Romas could assume that Korolenko was to play a significant role in Aleksei's development.

Romas engaged in revolutionary propaganda among the farmers. The store was only a front. He wanted to form a cooperative with the owners of small orchards to free them from the clutches of the large buyers. The landed gentry and the priest, however, created opposition wherever they could. One day in August the store and barn were burned down. Aleksei was almost killed when an oil barrel exploded while he was trying to rescue a trunk with books from the attic. He was very sad when he said goodbye to Romas, who was the only person in all that time to show any real interest in him. They did not meet again until fifteen years later in Sedlets.

After working for a while in the neighboring villages, Aleksei took a barge down the Volga to the Caspian Sea, where he found work in a fishery. A few weeks later, then twenty years old, he walked back to Kazan, crossing the Moskodian Steppe and the Shigulev Mountains.

Much had changed. Derenkov's bakery was closed and Aleksei found a job as night watchman at the solitary railroad station of Dobrinka. From six in the evening until six in the morning he watched warehouses, armed with a stick. After three months he was transferred to the freightyard of Borisoglebsk. His colleagues at work all belonged to the intelligentsia. They were former students, journalists, and officers under police surveillance for political "unreliability." The railroad administration employed them to fight the increasing number of thefts of cargoes. In the city the activities of the "politicals" were considered with suspicion, even hatred, and they were feared as the enemies of the czar and the people.

The story "The Night Watchman" describes life in Borisoglebsk:

I dreamed of various heroic deeds, of the joys of life while I had to guard sacks, coverings, ties, beams, and firewood. I had read Heine and Shakespeare; but when, during the night, I thought of reality, of all the putrefaction around me, then I sat or lay motionless by the hour, without understanding anything.

While the primitive and narrow-minded middle class of the small town only lived "in order to eat and accumulate provisions" and for the rest indulged in silly superstitions, the "good, clever intellectuals" spent their days in passive indifference. In their haughtiness they did not even realize the animosity of the bourgeois: "My intellect, my imagination, all my strength did not suffice to unite these two worlds, which were separated by the abyss of mutual estrangement." Thirty years later Gorki wrote in his memoirs:

The petrifying sensation of the spiritual isolation of the intelligentsia —as the rational principle—from the common people has haunted me all my life. The narration "My Travel Companion" and other stories have their root here. Gradually, this sensation changed into the premonition of a catastrophe. . . . If the dichotomy between the will and the intellect signifies a serious drama in the life of an individual, it becomes outright tragedy in the life of a people.

In the spring of 1889, Aleksei was transferred to the weighing station of Krutaya on the Volga-Don line. Life in this little station in the steppe passed "in boredom and silence," as we know from the story "The Book."

In his off-duty hours, Aleksei was surrounded by workers to whom he sometimes read pamphlets, at other times telling them about geography, history, and astronomy. He was an excellent narrator who knew how to hold his audience spellbound.

He and the telegraphist Yurin devoured everything readable "with insatiable greed, day and night": "In this desolate solitude the books offered views into

the world of active life." When within a short time
they had read all the books available at the six stations
between Volga and Don, they experienced "a period
of spiritual starvation. These tortures are known only
by those who have been close to suffocating in the
stifling boredom of our plains." As in Nishni he would
have liked to find refuge in a quiet corner to come to
terms with everything he had experienced. In this mood
he developed a tremendous enthusiasm for Tolstoi's
teachings and a desire to settle on the land.

Aleksei was almost twenty-one years old and he
had to report for military service. In May, he resigned
from his job with the railroads and traveled, on foot and
by hitchhiking, from Krutaya via Tambov, Ryasan,
Tula, and Moscow, to Nishni. It was his second journey
across Russia. In Moscow he wanted to speak with Lev
Tolstoi, but the author was not there. By the end of
September, Aleksei had reached Nishni and went to see
first of all the Narodnik writer Karonin, who energetically
proceeded to talk him out of his idea of forming an agri-
cultural colony. He was all the more successful because
of Aleksei's renewal of old acquaintances from Kazan.
With two of them, the former teacher Chekin and the
former student Somov, he moved into an apartment.
Both Chekin and Somov engaged in revolutionary activities and were under police surveillance. To make a living,
Aleksei worked as a coachman for a distributor of Bavar-
ian beer. He wore a hat with a wide brim, like bandits in
operas, the white jacket of a cook, the blue bulging trou-
sers of a policeman, and in this strange attire attracted
attention everywhere.

On October 12, 1889, the secret police in Nishni
were ordered on command from St. Petersburg to arrest
Somov. He, however, had disappeared. Although nothing suspicious was found when the apartment was

searched, Aleksei was brought up for interrogation. He behaved in a rather impudent, actually insolent manner, was arrested, and imprisoned for four weeks. The chief of the secret police started a brown file with the heading: "File of the police department, concerning the citizen Leksei Peshkov, November 1, 1889." The police chief believed that Aleksei's friendship with the much older roommates "led to the assumption that Peshkov was merely an instrument that Chekin and especially Somov used in order to spread or attempt to spread their opinions, which were inimical to the government." Information was collected from Kazan, Saratov, and Tsaritsyn on the subject of the "artisan of the painters' guild, Al. Peshkov." From Kazan came the information that Peshkov had not aroused any immediate suspicions as to his political attitudes, but that he had had contact with extremely suspicious characters. Because nothing could be proven against him and because all the other information spoke rather in his favor, he was released on November 8.

Major General Posnanski, who had conducted the investigation, enjoyed reading Aleksei's confiscated manuscripts and suggested that he show them to Korolenko and continue writing.

From the time of his first imprisonment, Aleksei Maksimovich was, as "politically unreliable," under police surveillance. For various reasons he was in a rather depressed mood. Because of his injured lung he had not passed the physical examinations of the draft board, and the topographic department of the army did not take him because of his political unreliability. Toward the end of 1889, he decided to follow Posnanski's advice and see Korolenko to show him his poetry and the poem "The Song of the Old Oak Tree."

Korolenko was widely known as a literary and political figure. The intelligentsia devoured his short stories and his novels; the officials and merchants were afraid of his scathing newspaper articles. The report of the secret police stated that his apartment in Nishni was a center for all politically unreliable persons. Korolenko leafed through the thick manuscript and finally tried, carefully, to show the young visitor how bad it was. "In our youth we all tend to be pessimists," he said. "I really don't know why. Apparently because we want so much and attain so little." This was exactly the mood in which "The Song of the Old Oak Tree" had been written.

Korolenko, with kind words, explained to Aleksei the faults in his style. This criticism was so devastating "that I no longer heard anything or understood anything and wanted only one thing: to run away." A few days later Korolenko returned the manuscript and wrote:

It is difficult to judge on the basis of the "Song" whether you have any talent or not. Write something you have experienced yourself and show it to me. I don't understand much about poems; yours seems incomprehensible, although it contains a few strong, impressive lines.

Aleksei tore up the manuscript in despair and burned it: "I decided never again to write verse or prose. And indeed, I did not write for two years, although at times I felt a strong urge to do so."

Fortunately, he could leave the hard job with the brewery and work as a secretary in the office of the lawyer A. I. Lanin. He was paid twenty rubles per month and something like order came into his life. Lanin took great interest in the intellectual development of his secretary, gave him his advice, and lent him his books.

As in Kazan, Aleksei visited the revolutionary circles in Nishni. Here he found the same passivity and lack of contact with the people, justified in endless debates.

The young man underwent another serious spiritual crisis. He attempted to solve his problems with the help of philosophy and became entangled in a web of contradictory ideas and tormenting doubts. He had accumulated a wealth of impressions and was not able to digest them:

I lacked the discipline or rather the technique of thinking, which only schooling provides. The narcotic of my books could no longer satisfy me. I was thirsting for a rational, truly great deed. With passionate zeal I collected the few crumbs of all that one could call unusual, good, selfless, beautiful.

In addition to all these difficulties, he encountered the excitement of first love when he met Olga Kaminskaya, the companion of the revolutionary Boveslav Korsak, who had just returned from exile; she was ten years older than Aleksei: "I was firmly convinced that only this woman was capable of bringing out in me the knowledge of my true identity." Olga, however, could not make up her mind to leave Korsak. "Partly ill and partly insane," Aleksei saw no alternative but to leave town. This leave turned into a two-year journey across Russia.

4

*Journeys
and First
Fame*

My journeys across Russia were not motivated by a desire to be a vagabond but to find out where I lived and what kind of people lived around me.

Aleksei traveled first along the Volga to Tsaritsyn: "I was so horrified at the stupidity and cruelty of man that it drove me almost insane." To find a solution to the burning question about the meaning of life and suffering, he visited several convents on the way. He hoped to find clarification from the hermits. Even the monks, however, could not give him a satisfactory answer or any consolation. He therefore, continued his travels through the Don valley to the Black Sea, stayed with farmers, helped fishermen, and worked in salt mines, on road constructions, and as a cargo hauler in the harbor of Odessa.

Late in 1891, he arrived in Tiflis. Here he met old friends: Mikhail Nachalov, whom he knew from Tsaritsyn, and Feodor Chaliapin, the former shoe-maker from Kazan whose life had also been quite adventurous. Chaliapin had traveled with a small theater company and had just been engaged at a miserable salary. Nachalov found a position for Aleksei as clerk with the railroad repair shops.

Aleksei moved in with the mechanic Afansyef and there also met the teacher Magalov and the locksmith Rokhlin. The four of them formed a "commune" and busily engaged in propaganda for the revolution. It was quite a lively group: young workers, teachers, and students read and debated; letters were exchanged with revolutionaries in other cities; and all of them constantly expected the appearance of the "Shiny Buttons"—the police.

Aleksei's activities were not very intense. In a letter he remarked: "I am sure I was a fantast and poetaster at the time, but my usefulness as propagandist was probably quite limited." Contemporaries remember that he had a notebook filled with poems, a head filled with plans, and that he was specially enamored of Byron, whose poems kept the spirit of protest and dissatisfaction awake in him.

The journeys had soothed his tormented state of mind, even though the experiences had not always been enjoyable. At least he felt more secure of himself than in former times. In addition, the people with whom he associated exerted a positive influence on him.

The acquaintance with Aleksander Kalyushny was to prove of special significance. In the 1870's, Kalyushny had been condemned to six years of forced labor. He had the rare gift of attracting people, searching their souls and finding out the way of life that would be best for them. When most of the students and teachers left the city during the summer of 1892, the "commune" was dissolved and Kalyushny asked Aleksei to move in with him. Aleksei thus finally found the peace and quiet that he needed. The daily contact with the host led to a deep friendship. Kalyushny owned a good library and interested the young man in the Russian and foreign classical authors. He suggested, however, that Aleksei abandon arithmetic and cosmography, as well as Nietzsche and Schopenhauer. Gorki wrote his friend in 1925:

You were the first person who saw in me not merely a young man with a rather strange biography, a wandering vagabond, an interesting, but nevertheless dubious individual. I still remember your eyes when you heard me telling you about my experiences and myself. I understood then that one could never brag in front of you and thanks to you I never suffered from any exaggerated self-esteem and I never even exaggerated all the sadness life had so richly bestowed on me. You were the first who helped me to take myself seriously, who treated me truly like a human being.

Kalyushny, who believed unwaveringly in the talent of his protégé, suggested that he write every-

thing down just as he had seen and experienced it.
Aleksei was a good and interesting narrator, but his
style became dull when he tried to write anything down.
Lines of books that he had read intruded themselves
and he wrote strange words, imitating the writing of
others. As a result everything sounded false. Over and
over again Kalyushny asked him to write down the
story of Loyko and Radda that Aleksei had heard
from the old horse guard Makar Chudra in a gypsy
camp—the legend of a people with an immense desire
for freedom. Finally "Makar Chudra" was written
down as Aleksei had absorbed it, woven out of his
own impressions and dreams.

Then he was again seized with the desire to travel.
He journeyed along the Black Sea to the Kuban region,
where he became involved in the so-called "plague
rebellion" and was put in jail as a vagabond. The people
had rebelled against the senseless measures taken by
czarist officials to fight the cattle plague and had beaten
these officials; the cossacks were then brought in,
retaliating in the bloodiest fashion. Aleksei worked
again with the railroads for a while, and by fall was
back in Tiflis. This short period provided material
for such later stories as "Caucasian Robbers," "In
the Gorge," "Strangers," and "The Woman."

Kalyushny had in the meantime succeeded in
placing "Makar Chudra" with the important Tiflis
paper *Caucasus.* Only the name of the author was
still missing, and with great deliberation Aleksei
Maksimovich signed it as Gorki, which means "the
Bitter One." The literary career of Maksim Gorki
begins with the printing of this first narration in
September of 1892.

Enormously encouraged, he immediately wrote
another story, "From the Life of a Prostitute." The

editor of *Caucasus* returned the manuscript, however, stating the material seemed "inappropriate and compromising."

That autumn proved especially happy for Aleksei, who was then twenty-four years old. Olga Kaminskaya had returned from Paris and separated from Korsak. She was moved by the unaltered affection of the young man, who in the meantime had changed for the better. They decided on a life together. He accepted an offer that his former employer Lanin sent him by telegram, and in October he returned by Volga steamer to Nishni.

In December, Olga moved with him into an old bathhouse that he had rented from the priest. He lived in the anteroom, while the bathroom proper was Olga's and served at the same time as guestroom. It was bitterly cold. When he worked at night, he wrapped himself up in all the clothes he owned plus a rug. During that period he contracted rheumatism. Olga made hats for ladies in the city, painted portraits, and designed maps. During the day, Gorki wrote applications and petitions for appeal and went to court for his employer. At night he read Balzac and philosophy in his "cabinet."

He also worked hard on new stories and dreamed of distant voyages. They never had any money and sometimes even owed the two rubles a month for rent: "At that time, I still did not believe that I could ever become a serious writer; working for the newspaper was only a means of making a living . . . ." Olga was not interested in his writings. Whenever he read to her, she fell asleep.

He was fortunate, however, in finding a new friend and teacher, just as he had found Smury, Romas, Lanin, and Kalyushny. This was Korolenko, who had read Gorki's poem "The Song of the Old Oak Tree" in 1889. Korolenko was the first friend to impress on Gorki the significance of form, and thanks to him the future writer worked to cultivate a plain and simple style.

Almost an entire year elapsed before he again sent something to a newspaper. When a Moscow journal published his novella *Yemalyan Pilyay* in August, he became more self-confident and sent several stories to the most influential paper of the Volga valley, the *Volshski Vestnik.* All the stories were accepted. The best known was "The Siskin that Lied." Soon after that, the Nishni-Novgorod journal *Volgar* published little sketches and stories by Gorki.

Korolenko followed all the publications of his protégé with great attention, and early in 1894 he advised him to write something larger for a periodical, because Aleksei had developed beyond the stage of provincial papers. Within two days, Gorki wrote "Chelkash," the story of a well-known smuggler who had occupied the bed next to Aleksei's in the hospital in Nikolayev and who had wanted to hire Aleksei. Korolenko was enthusiastic:

You know how to draw characters; they speak and act on their own, out of their own inner being. You understand the art of not interfering in their thoughts and emotions. Not every writer can boast this gift! Your great talent consists in presenting people just as they are. I have always told you, you are a realist.

Then he thought for a moment and added: "But you are also a romantic." Korolenko took it upon himself to place the story in a distinguished periodical and after a few changes "Chelkash" was published in 1895.

Korolenko not only supervised and helped Gorki's literary activities; he was also instrumental in bringing order into Gorki's life. Because Gorki's income had increased and Olga liked to have many people around her, frequent "banquets" were given in the bathhouse. Gorki did not like these loud festivities; he wanted to write and read in tranquillity. Rumor and gossip about more and more turbulent and less and less pleasant conditions reached Korolenko, who told Gorki: "You absolutely have to get away from here. You have to begin a new life! I have a good friend at a Samara newspaper; I shall send him a few lines and he will give you a job."

Gorki knew that Korolenko was right; Olga too saw that a separation was necessary. He remembered their parting many years later in the sketch "My First Love": "We embraced warmly and were both quiet and sad for a while—then I left the city. She left soon after me to become an actress. So ended my first love. Despite its bad ending it was a beautiful story."

Gorki always remained in contact with his fatherly teacher. The portrait "Vladimir Korolenko" gives proof of the deep gratitude and veneration Gorki felt throughout his life for the selfless and helpful friend who had so decisively influenced his spiritual and literary development.

In February 1895, Gorki moved to Samara and became editor of the *Samarskaya Gazeta*. For a hundred rubles a month he had to write a daily feuilleton; he received three kopecks per line for literary contributions. Although he complained about the daily pressure, the feuilletons provided good stylistic exercises: they forced him to be short and realistic. His apartment was in a dark, humid basement close to the Volga. With its empty white walls, the sparse light falling from above, and the Spartan iron bed, it resembled the cell of a monk. Books were scattered everywhere, on the table, on the chair, next to the bed, on the floor.

Gorki's next long work was a series of stories published in the Sunday edition of the paper under the general title *Shadow Images*. Among them were "The Song of the Falcon," later to become so famous, "The Excursion," "Old Isergil," "An Error," and "The Raftsmen."

As a publisher, he believed it to be his task "to hunt in the dark undergrowth of our ignorance the beasts of stupidity and un-culture and to shoot them expertly." Under the pseudonym of Yehudiel Klamida he investigated the price of cattle and bacon; he fought the rich people of the town and the officials of the railroad administration, who defrauded their employees unscrupulously; and he attacked large buyers out to cheat the farmers, as well as the storeowners who exploited their apprentices. He cared especially about the social injustices. He became the speaker for the part of urban society that had no voice. His attacks were usually very sharp, so that even Korolenko found fault with their crudeness: "Even though you may reprimand all these people for good reason, you must not lose your sense of proportion and propriety." Still more upset about Klamida was the competing newspaper *Vestnik,* which accused him of having "crawled around with barefoot tramps in garbage dumps" and warned that in his aggressive tone he conjured up the danger of a "disintegration of the press." They made fun of his inclination to romanticism and were shocked by the erotic element in his stories.

Gorki was very much alone; he had few friends. His stories from that time are definitely pessimistic. The dull life of the provincial town almost suffocated him. "I was discontent with the governor, the bishop, the city, the entire world, with myself, and much else."

Early in 1896, Gorki married Yekaterina Pavlovna Volshina, who was a proofreader at the *Samarskaya Gazeta* and ten years younger than he. She was a dedicated revolutionary and a typical intellectual. They had two children: the son Maksim Alekseyevich (born in 1897) and the daughter Yekaterina, who was born in 1901 and died five years later of tuberculosis. On May 14, the couple moved to Nishni, where Gorki joined the paper *Nishegorodski Listok.*

During this period the city was preparing for the Pan-Russian Industrial Exhibition, designed to show to Europe the economic progress of the country and with it the success and power of czarism. Here Gorki wrote "In the Steppes," "Konovalov," "Creatures That Once Were Men," as well as feuilletons on the exhibition and various other topics. He participated with special interest in the discussions of the various art movements and vehemently fought against naturalism and decadence. He maintained that the naturalists "confined themselves to a protocol-like rendition of life" and that by explaining man's actions in terms of biological laws they concentrated exclusively on the baseness of human nature. In the sketch "The Reader," which in content resembles Nekrasov's poem "The Poet and the Citizen," he expounded the principles of his aesthetics in the form of a dialogue between reader and author:

It is the goal of literature to help man to understand himself better, to strengthen his faith in himself, and to guide him in his search for the Good.

In 1896, a book by Sologub, a co-founder of the Russian Decadence, was published. Gorki reviewed it under the significant title "Still Another Poet" and in this review sketched the characteristics of the decadent movement:

Pessimism and total indifference toward reality; the passionate drive toward the beyond, any place away from this world, into heaven; the awareness of a lack of strength; the absence of a sacred enthusiasm; all these are the main themes and the core of the new poetry.

In the articles "Paul Verlaine and the Decadents" he states:

These songs of a disintegrating culture sound like the dirges for a hypertense, mentally exhausted, egotistical society and sap all remaining strength. Decadence is a harmful, asocial phenomenon and needs to be fought.

To counter this "decadence in the arts" he favored the classics and the oral folkloric tradition that he had loved since his early childhood, because they "rendered life truthfully, awakened in man the most precious feelings and thoughts, and incited him to fight his oppressors." In these years are to be found the beginnings of the new art movement that he founded. This movement later hardened into the so-called socialist realism, although Gorki had conceived of it as a humanistic realism.

During the single year of 1896, Gorki wrote more than two hundred feuilletons, forty-one stories, and numerous reviews and short essays. The hunger, poverty, and hard work of his childhood, his restless life, the bullet through his lung, and finally the excessive literary activities—all led to the tuberculosis that he contracted in October 1896. In December his physician sent him to the Crimea. From the spring of 1897 he lived in the quiet Ukrainian village Manuylovka, where his condition gradually improved. He founded a village theater and also acted in it. In this country peace and solitude he wrote a series of stories, including "The Good-for-Nothing," "Malva," "The Fair at Goltva," "Orloff and His Wife." When winter approached he returned to Nishni and resumed work at the newspaper. On May 6, 1898, his house was suddenly searched and he was taken to jail. His photograph had been found in the apartment of his former roommate Afansyef in Tiflis and the police files stated: "Peshkov is an extremely dangerous person, because he is well read and puts his pen to good use. He has traveled on foot through nearly all of Russia and for a while lived for reasons unknown with the barge haulers of the Volga." On May 11, Gorki was sent to the political section of the prison at Metekh Castle in Tiflis, but he was released on May 21. The proceedings against him continued for an entire year and were then abandoned "on the very highest authority."

A few days before his imprisonment, the first volume of his collected stories had appeared, soon to be followed by a second volume. Both volumes were out of print within a few months. A new edition in three volumes similarly sold out very rapidly. In a short time his stories had sold 100,000 copies—something unheard of until then. The reasons for this tremendous success are to be found, on the one hand, in the political conditions of the period. Reactionary repression had followed the desperate fights of the nihilists in the 1870's. After the attempted assassination of Aleksander II, thousands of young and gifted people had been sent to Siberia. Profound pessimism spread, paralyzing all hope and progress. Side by side with a degenerate aristocracy, a wealthy bourgeoisie was rising. The progressing industrialization engendered a new social stratum, the proletariat, which was composed above all of small farmers and the lower classes of the cities. All the great Russian authors of that period, such as Dostoevski, Tolstoi, or Chekhov, portrayed despairing people, filled with a tormented longing for a better and more meaningful life, yet lacking the strength for an act of liberation and therefore doomed to disintegration. Gorki, however, affirmed life with all his strength, and he was not ready to settle for the existing conditions.

He rejected the "theory of the salvation of the soul through suffering," believing that "Russia had borne enough pain and sorrow." His revolutionary-romantic heroes are strong, selfless, noble men, ready to fight for the happiness of the people and the triumph of justice.

In November 1898, Gorki sent his books to Anton Chekhov:

I would like to confess to you my most sincere and warmest love—a love that has accompanied me since childhood. I would like to express to you my highest esteem of your genius, which is full of sadness and touches the soul, which is tragic and tender and always so beautiful and fine. How many wonderful moments have I experienced through your works and how often have I cried over them. . . .

With this letter began a cordial and creative friendship that was further deepened when the two met in Yalta.

Gorki met another outstanding contemporary, Lev Tolstoi, in January 1900. Tolstoi entered in his diary: "Gorki was here. We had a good conversation and I like him. He is a man truly from among the people."

By 1899, Gorki was already famous. He was writing for such distinguished papers as the Marxist *Novoye Slovo,* the *Ruskaya Mysl,* and *Shisn.* He also turned to other literary forms. *Shisn* published his first long novel, *Foma Gordeyev,* in which he most strikingly portrayed the Russian bourgeoisie: overbearing in its economic success, deprived of all moral standards, and totally dedicated to profit. The human destinies are embedded in the magnificent descriptions of nature that enhance many of Gorki's works. One year later his second novel, *Three of Them,* was finished. In it, a petty bourgeois, who strives only for his own profit, is confronted with a worker fighting for socialism.

In addition to all his literary activities, Gorki dedicated himself to tasks of a social and cultural nature. Many people came to see him and to speak with him. His two-story house in his native city was constantly beleaguered. Among his visitors were a few police agents who kept Gorki and all his friends under surveillance. Every visitor had a new request:

One wants a book; the other suffers from a longing to write poetry. A printer returns from exile; the wife of the governor brings illegal brochures; a seamstress is looking for a job; the local commander asks for a special theater performance for his soldiers; a merchant invites you to a discussion on God. . . .

Gorki took care of them all and helped wherever he could. He also remembered the poor children of Nishni, for whom he collected presents, and the barge haulers, for whom he set up a day center, complete with library and piano.

The agents were specially upset because Gorki often went to the manufacturing suburb of Sormovo. The workers frequently came to him as well, asking for books, advice, or the money they needed for their revolutionary activities. The once-secret workers' circles had united in 1898 to form the Russian Social Democratic Workers' Party, and their rank and file already contained the future leaders of the Bolsheviks; Lenin's first mimeographed articles were distributed in these factories. The social democratic newspaper *Iskra* was also published in Sormovo; Lenin was on its staff. The newspaper was printed on thin rice paper, so that it could be chewed and swallowed in case of sudden police raids.

5

"Firebird" of the Revolution

On March 17, 1901 (then March 4), the famous student demonstration took place in front of the Kazan cathedral in St. Petersburg. Gorki saw how the cossacks attacked the demonstrators and cut them down pitilessly. Outraged by these brutalities, he, along with many others, signed a protest that had been drafted by the federation of authors. At the same time, *Shisn* published Gorki's "The Song of the Firebird," in which he openly showed his sympathy for the impending revolution. Like "The Song of the Falcon" (1895), it is a symbolic verse allegory. The revolutionary youth groups learned the lines by heart. While "The Song of the Falcon" portrayed a single fighter who succumbed in the unequal struggle, the "Firebird" anticipated the mass movements on the eve of the first revolution. It has been labeled "the purest expression of the romantic revolutionary spirit" with which Gorki's entire work is imbued.

In April, Gorki and many other like-minded people were jailed. Among them was his future adopted son, Sinovi Moisevich Sverdlov. All were accused of having put a mimeograph machine, which they bought in St. Petersburg, at the disposal of the workers in Sormovo. Gorki was treated as a dangerous criminal. He was indicted for his contacts with revolutionary Social Democrats and for public instigations to riot during the Kazan demonstrations. Gorki's arrest and imprisonment caused a wave of protest all over Russia, led by Lev Tolstoi. A council consisting of seven physicians found evidence of new tuberculosis in Gorki; he was released under house arrest in May. He was then in a position, however, to continue his support of the revolutionaries of the *Iskra* circle. According to police records, he contributed 5,000 rubles, spending scarcely a third of his royalties on personal matters.

The police, "in the interest of public order," soon proclaimed his presence in Nishni an inconvenience, and he was therefore banished to Arsamas, a dull little provincial town. He petitioned for permission to live in the Crimean, and because of his ill health the petition was granted, provided that he would stay near Yalta, but not in the city itself, until April 15, 1902. When he left on November 1, 1901, the young revolutionary intelligentsia of Nishni, comprising students and workers, used his departure to stage a lively demonstration. They sang the *Marseillaise,* distributed pamphlets, and marched through the streets, shouting, "Long live the revolutionary poet Maksim Gorki! Long live freedom!" Describing this event, Gorki later wrote to his publisher W. A. Posse: "The police were in a state of confusion and were smart enough not to undertake anything."

In the Crimea, Gorki led a relatively quiet life. He wrote much. From earlier letters to Chekhov we know that even in Nishni he had begun to work on a play, *The Petty Bourgeois,* inspired by a performance of Chekhov's *Uncle Vanya.* Gorki was a daily guest of Chekhov. "Almost the entire elite of Russian literature" met at the famous playwright's house, as Stanislavski remembered in his memoirs. At that time Stanislavski and the actors of the Moscow Art Theater had an engagement at the Little Theater in Yalta, and they performed plays by Chekhov every evening.

Gorki was not used to the dramatic form and work did not progress easily. He wrote, made changes, rewrote. "I don't like it," he told Chekhov. "During the winter months, I shall most certainly write another play, and if that does not turn out, ten more; but I shall reach what I set out for! The play must be full of harmony and beauty, like music." When Stanislavski urged him to finish the play in a hurry because he wanted to perform it in his theater, Gorki confessed to him what a hard time he had with the characters in the play:

They always surround me, push me and coerce me; yet I cannot place them, cannot find my position among them, really! They talk and talk and what they say is not even bad, so that it is all the more a pity that one has to interrupt them.

In a letter dated February 26, 1902, the chairman of the section for Russian language and literature of the Academy of Sciences informed Gorki that the Academy had made him an honorary member. This election elicited outraged responses from government circles and the reactionaries. It was called "a mockery to all talent," and "an insult to the two hundred years of the existence of our academy." Gorki was mischievously labeled a "two-week academician" and an "academically premature delivery." The czar wrote to the minister of public education: "I am most profoundly disturbed that the Academy dares to elect such an individual in these troubled and restless times." Thereupon Gorki was asked to return his letter of appointment. Only two members of the Academy protested Gorki's expulsion and in their turn resigned from the honor of being members of the Academy. They were Anton Chekhov and Vladimir Korolenko.

All these disturbances hardly upset Gorki, and they did not damage his popularity—very much to the contrary. On the occasion of a guest performance of the Moscow Art Theater in St. Petersburg, and after strict censorship, *The Petty Bourgeois* was performed on March 26, 1902. The government feared demonstrations, and even during dress rehearsal the theater was surrounded by regular and mounted police. At the world premiere, the ushers too were replaced by policemen. In the play, Gorki portrayed the people he had known all his life—the lower middle class in their small houses stuffed with samovars, icons, and trunks—and he called on the Russian people to participate actively in transforming their lives. The figure of the train conductor Nil embodied the revolutionary worker of the future as Gorki saw him.

The premiere was only a moderate success. Despite the efforts of the actors, the author's social criticism did not reach the audience, probably because of the rigorous deletions. In contrast, the premieres in Berlin and Vienna, which took place in December of the same year, were more successful.

In addition to *The Petty Bourgeois,* Gorki had been working on a second play, *The Lower Depths,* dealing with barefoot tramps. He knew the heroes of his play from the roads and harbors. He had slept with them on narrow cots or sat up with them around camp fires. The figure of Satin, for example, was modeled on a former postal employee who had been committed to forced labor. Many earlier stories appear to be sketches for this drama. The flophouse of the former cavalry major Kuvalda in "Creatures That Once Were Men" recalls Kostylyov's place in *The Lower Depths* in many respects. One difference, however, needs to be stressed: Gorki had formerly endowed these outcasts with the traits of romantic heroes in order "to bring some beauty through imagination into the oppressively poor life." He had done this to thank these tramps for the small favors they had done him in his journeys through the squalors of daily life in Russia. In this work, however, he had the courage to speak the bitter truth about people who vegetate in flophouses and wander about in utter despair. In *The Lower Depths* he did not present noble and picturesque heroes in the fashion of Chelkash, but people who have been mercilessly squelched by life, oppressed by the feeling that no one needs them—the outcasts. Gorki did this not to incite pity and compassion, but out of his hatred of a society that can push people to the bottom of life.

The people of *The Lower Depths* vegetate in a cave-like basement that serves as a setting for the misery of human depravity. Alcohol, gambling, beatings, and the memory of better days fill the days and nights. The pilgrim Luka carries an intimation of a better world into this darkness; he is full of kindness and humane feelings and the desire to help. He disappears, however, and the dream of a change that he had awakened in some of the people vanishes. Here Satin speaks about an appreciation of man, a motif appears that runs through all of Gorki's writing:

If anything great and sacred exists in this world, it is most certainly man on his journey of progressive growth; and this man is no less precious if I should not like him.

Gorki personally read *The Lower Depths* in September 1902, in the presence of Chirikov, Nadyenov, Chaliapin, and the actors of the Moscow Art Theater. At the point where Luka administers the sacrament of Holy Communion to the dying Anna and consoles her, everyone stopped breathing. A great silence followed; Gorki's voice began to shake and then broke. He wiped away a tear; he wanted to continue to read, but after two words he stopped again and began to cry.

The actors started their rehearsals enthusiastically. They studied their new heroes and tried to familiarize themselves with their lives. Gorki told them about his years of wandering and about the people that had served as models for his characters; he imitated their gestures and related details about their mode of living. To observe the conditions in an actual flophouse, the troupe

went to the notorious Khitrov market, a dissolute neigh-
borhood in Moscow: "We saw the wide dormitories with
innumerable cots, on which many old people—men as
well as women—lay stretched out like the dead." When
Stanislavski told these people his reason for being there,
"the vagabonds were so moved they started to cry." The
main result of this excursion was that the director understood the value of the play: "Freedom at any price . . .
that kind of freedom for which people let themselves fall
to the lowest depths of life without realizing that there
they will turn into slaves."

The world premiere of the play—which in a strict
sense is not a drama but a loose sequence of scenes—
took place on December 18, 1902. It moved the audience
not only through its artistic representation of suffering,
but above all because it expressed faith in a more digni-
fied future for the Russian people. Even during the first
act Gorki was called out, and at the end of the play the
ovations reached unprecedented intensity. The newspapers scarcely found words for such an overwhelming
success. The conservatives recognized the revolutionary
stance only too clearly, even though it was presented in a
romantic-rebellious vein. They instigated and agitated
until any performance of the play in the provinces was
forbidden. In St. Petersburg, however, by April 1903 the
play had been performed fifty times to sold-out houses.
Gorki's adversaries, moreover, could not keep him from
being awarded the Griboyedov prize. He was the hero
of the day. Wherever he appeared, male and especially
female groups of admirers congregated and stared at him
until he became embarrassed; his helpless embarrassment
only increased the enthusiasm of his admirers.

As early as January 23, 1903, *The Lower Depths*
became one of Max Reinhardt's most impressive suc-
cesses. On May 5, 1905, the five-hundredth performance

was given. A grateful Gorki wrote to Reinhardt on
August 1, 1903:

Nothing unites people as much as art. May art live and with her all
those who serve her faithfully, without hesitating to present the hard
truth about life as it is! I most heartily embrace you and your artists!
I deeply regret that I do not speak the German language and am
ashamed of my ignorance. . . .

After its performance in Berlin *The Lower Depths,*
with its indictment of the czarist regime, was performed
throughout the world. In Russia, it served as the literary
prologue to the revolutions of 1905 and 1917.

When Gorki's third play, *The Summer Guests,* was
first performed in St. Petersburg on November 11, 1904,
all the leading literary and journalistic figures were present. Although the revolutionary intelligentsia enthusiastically applauded the author, the members of the
czarist regime vainly attempted to disturb the performance by whistling and hissing during the third act. The
play treated

. . . purely Russian family matters. . . . I wanted to portray the part
of the Russian intelligentsia that had come from the democratic strata
and after having reached a certain social status lost the connection
with the people to which it was related and forgot their interests.

The conservative intelligentsia completely withdrew from
Gorki after they had seen this play; they were disappointed and angered, because he had held a mirror to their
weakness and impotence.

Gorki's financial situation was very good at that
time. After 1900 he was a member of the publishing
house Snaniye, which had been founded on completely
new principles by K. P. Pyatnitski in 1898. All the authors were partners. After a small deduction for organi-
zational expenditures they received the entire income
from the sale of their books. Gorki attracted the best

literary talents of his times to this venture, and through
his initiative the publishing house became the center for
all revolutionary democratic literature. The first four-
volume edition of his stories was published by this firm,
and between 1904 and 1913 forty volumes of the tremendously successful "Anthologies of the Snaniye
Company" appeared. Such writers as Chekhov, Serafi-
movich, Veresayev, Kuprin, Bunin, and Skitalets co-
operated in this enterprise.

Gorki was then in a position to carry out his con-
cepts of a new, realistic art:

All around us, a new life begins to pulsate, stimulating a new awareness, and with it a new man is born. He is more eager to know, thirsting for books, demanding an answer to the fundamental questions
of life and the mind. He wants to know where to find truth and justice,
where to find friends, and who the enemy is.

The principles of the publishing house were to be
"democratism and positivism":

The more I live and think, read and see, the more I am convinced that
it is not imagination or dreams that conquer the horrors of life, but
experience, the storing of experience, and its well-balanced organization.

As far as the decision depended on him, no pessimists should be published by the Snaniye. His animosity
against "all modes of expressing the psychic disintegration of personality in Russian literature" became
increasingly belligerent, and in 1908 he demanded in
a letter to Pyatnitski that their house "ought to combat
all that rabble—those Ivanov-Rasumniks, Mereshkov-
skis, Struves, Sologubs, Kusmins, and so forth."

In 1904 the czarist army suffered defeat after
defeat, and rebellion and resistance among the workers
increased daily. These desperate people conceived
the naive plan of going to the czar and asking him for

help. On January 9, 1905, under the leadership of the priest Gabon, 200,000 men, women and children marched to the Winter Palace, where they wished to hand a petition to the czar. The petition read:

We have come to you, our monarch, seeking truth and protection. Despotism and arbitrariness are strangling us. . . . For us that horrible moment has come when death is more desirable than the continuation of our unbearable suffering.

Although the government was aware of the peaceful nature of the demonstration, the troops suddenly fired into the unarmed masses. "It was a premeditated massacre, staged in grandiose terms," Gorki wrote to his wife. "The Russian revolution has begun."

He then drafted an "Appeal to All Russian Citizens and to the Public Opinion of All European States," calling the horrendous events that he had witnessed plain murder and holding the czar responsible for them. The manuscript fell into the hands of the police. On January 11, Gorki was arrested and taken to the Peter-Paul Fortress, the prison for the most important political criminals. The indictment stated that "the artisan A. M. Peshkov had drawn up an appeal with the purpose of promulgating it, instigating the overthrow of the present political and social structure." He was supposed to be tried behind closed doors.

The response to Gorki's arrest was an enormous wave of protest, not only in Russia, but in foreign countries as well. Under the heading of "Save Gorki," the Berlin papers *Vorwärts* and *Berliner Tagesblatt* of January 28 passionately demanded a human and just judgment of the author, whose destiny soon became a concern for the entire intellectual and artistic world. Known politicians and artists signed the petition and the list of names grew. On the other hand, the papers voicing the opinion of the government and the Catholic press, such as the *Neue Preussische Kreuzzeitung, Germania,* and *Kölnische Zeitung,* refused to plead for Gorki's release, declaring that they did not wish to interfere in the purely domestic policies of another country. All over Europe, however, noted figures championed Gorki. Anatole France asserted: "Gorki belongs not only to Russia, but to the entire world." Pierre Curie, Auguste Rodin, Jean Jaurès, Claude Monet, and many other prominent persons joined him. Even the Portuguese king, Dom Pedro, interceded on behalf of the "poet of the revolution." In the Metropolitan Theater in New York *The Lower Depths* was performed with a prelude, showing the author writing in his cell. The Russian newspapers constantly published the foreign petitions, and in the paper *Novosti* thousands of voices united in the claim:

Release Maksim Gorki to his work, to his country, to the entire world! Humanity intercedes for him. . . . A harsh judgment or long imprisonment could deprive Russia and the entire cultured world of a creative genius from whom much is still expected.

In the meantime and after many requests, Gorki was granted "utensils to continue his literary activities," and far from losing his courage, he wrote a new play, *Children of the Sun,* which he called a "gay comedy." The guards often heard him laugh out loud during his writing. Surprised, they informed the commander of the fortress of these inappropriate outbursts of happiness. The commander went to see Gorki—and stayed for hours, conversing with him.

Again the government—for the third time—was obliged to yield, and in February 1905 Gorki was released on bail of 10,000 rubles. His health had suffered considerably during his imprisonment and he and his family were given permission to go to Yalta. He did not stay there very long, however; on May 15, he went to Kuokkala in Finland.

In August, the newspapers reported that the censors had prohibited the performance of his play *The Barbarians* in all of Russia. The performances of *The Children of the Sun* in St. Petersburg and other cities ended, without exception, in riots.

The czar, pressured by the revolutionary events of the Bloody Sunday in St. Petersburg, published a manifesto on October 17, in which he promised the people "unalienable principles of civic freedom." This decree allowed, on October 27, the publication of the first edition of *Novaya Shisn,* the first Marxist newspaper in Russia, edited by Lenin. It was financed by Maksim Gorki and Maria Fyodorovna Andreyeva. The former actress and future companion of the author in his exile had visions that in this paper "the best poems, the best stories of the times, and the most passionate political articles" should be published. On the staff were among others Lunacharski, Maslov, Andreyev, Balmont, Chirikov, as well as the foreign Social Democrats Karl Kautsky, Karl Liebknecht, and Rosa Luxemburg. The very first number was confiscated. The editorial board protested the "assault on a Social Democratic newspaper," but the confiscations were continued until, on December 2, *Novaya Shisn* had to suspend publication. Before that date, however, the paper managed to print such material as Lenin's famous article "Party Organization and Party Literature" and Gorki's "Remarks on the Petty Bourgeoisie," directed against the antirevolutionary spirit of the Russian intelligentsia.

During all these months Gorki, then living in Moscow, worked indefatigably for the revolution by giving speeches and writing articles. He collected money for the impending insurrection, claiming, "I need the money for boots," by which he meant weapons, which he then stacked in his apartment. In St. Petersburg on November 27 he met Lenin for the first time. The armed insurrection in Moscow began on December 9, and Gorki was full of praise for the splendid attitude of the workers. In his letter of December 10 to Pyatnitski he stated soberly: "The winner will of course be the government, but not for long . . . and they will have to pay dearly for their victory."

Gorki was right: the uprising was suppressed with great bloodshed. In a mimeographed pamphlet to the workers, distributed all over Russia, Gorki called out to them:

The proletariat is not vanquished, although it has suffered losses. The revolution is strengthened with new hope. The Russian workers have embarked on the road to final victory, because they are the only morally strong class-conscious strata in Russia that believe in their own future.

The czarist government planned to alleviate its chronic lack of money through loans from abroad. When this decision was made, the Central Committee of the Russian Social-Democratic Workers' Party proceeded to use the world fame of the author for its own purposes. Gorki would travel to the foreign countries and there spread the truth about the revolution in Russia, he would attempt to interfere with the granting of loans to the czarist government through enlightening lectures and articles, and he would collect donations for the party.

Toward the end of January 1906, Gorki wrote to his wife from a "secret place" in Finland where he was hiding from an impending arrest. In the letter he said that he would only return when "better times have come; the authorities make it clearly known that they want to get hold of me. I am not interested in being in jail and therefore I shall go abroad."

In February, he arrived in Berlin, where he met Bebel, Kautsky, Liebknecht, and of course Max Reinhardt. The Moscow Art Theater was on tour there, and Gorki was well known for his plays *The Petty Bourgeois, Children of the Sun,* and above all, *The Lower Depths.* The Russian secret police had vainly attempted to bar his traveling permit; they could only keep him under close surveillance.

The modest writer, who was little given to public honors, continued his travels incognito to Switzerland, then via Paris and Cherbourg to New York, where he was honored with a "particularly triumphal and noisy reception": "For forty-eight hours the New York press could speak of nothing but me and the purpose of my trip." After three days, however, the wave of enthusiasm subsided. The Russian Okhrana (secret police) had done its work. They had made files available to the immigration office and the American press, stating that Gorki was an "anarchist and bigamist." His companion, M. F. Andreyevna, was not his legal wife and, they said, his family in Russia was starving. New York society rose in protest against the "moral depravity" of the writer: "I was thrown out of three hotels and everybody withdrew from me. I found lodgings with an American author and waited to see what was going to happen. The newspapers began to discuss the necessity of expelling me from the country." The most influential papers, however, had already placed him under contract for writing articles and did not participate in this slander against him. Things gradually returned to normal, and Gorki could begin his campaign against loans to Russia from the West. His main argument consisted in pointing out that the czar would misuse the credit in the attempt to suppress the revolutionary movement further. His appeals to public opinion awakened concern and donations came in large quantities.

Gorki studied American life with great attention and interest and reported his impressions in the realistic sketches *In America* and in pamphlets:

I have seen a great deal of poverty, I know its greenish, bloodless, bony face. Yet the horror of the poverty of the East Side is worse than anything I know. . . . These streets are crowded with people as if they were flour sacks; the children search in garbage cans along the streets for rotten vegetables and devour right then and there whatever they find, including the mildew. The dust bites and the humidity is unbearable. To find a small crust of bread incites the wildest animosities among the children and they fight like dogs to get hold of the piece of bread. They cover the roads in clusters like voracious pigeons. At one o'clock in the morning, at two, and even later, they still wallow in the filth—those miserable microbes of poverty.

In these words from "The City of the Yellow Devil" he expressed his revulsion over the extremely depressing conditions that accompany Western capitalism. Not less aggressive are his *Interviews,* short satirical conversations with such figures as Kaiser Wilhelm, Czar Nicholas, and the "American King."

When the French government decided to grant the czar the requested loan, Gorki wrote the famous-infamous pamphlet *Beautiful France,* which ends:

France! The greed for gold has brought you to shame! Your connections with the bankers have spoiled your honorable soul. . . . You, mother of freedom, you, Jeanne d'Arc, have come to the succour of beasts so that they can try once more to strangle man. . . . Your gold makes it possible once more for the blood of the Russian people to flow. Once upon a time I loved you. Today I spit blood and bile into your face!

The French papers were shocked by this "totally crazy essay" and reproached the writer for being ungrateful. The reactionary "Pelerin" wrote: "Until recently our press made a lot of fuss over the Russian revolutionary Maksim Gorki and praised his work highly. . . . Now he is busy defiling France in disgusting articles . . ." The historian A. Aulard concluded: "To spit at France is the gesture of a sick man, drunk on ink." The French leftist papers, which were all against the loan, reminded the writer how eagerly cultured France had read his works and risen in his defense. Gorki replied to these accusations only when he was back in Europe.

In the article Gorki prepared for the socialist newspaper *L'Humanité* on December 11, 1906, he wrote:

I know that an entire people is never responsible for the politics of the dominating classes and their obedient lackeys, the government. The people is always betrayed and abused by the leaders of its destiny, be they Germans, Englishmen, or Frenchmen, kings, bankers, or journalists. I have spit in the face of the France of the banks and financiers, the France of the police forces and the ministries, which has defamed Émile Zola, which out of fear . . . has drowned all honorable feelings and is finally reduced to trembling for the stability of the franc.

Gorki's revolutionary agitation in the United States made a return to Russia under the present power structure impossible. He had been a member of the Social Democratic Party since his release from the prison fortress in February 1905 and, because of his revolutionary activities, was an object of special concern for the Russian government. Even before the December revolution, he had not dared to see his family at Yalta, being afraid for his life. He had stayed in Moscow. "There are fewer chances here of getting murdered . . ." he wrote to his wife on October 24, 1905.

Seeking a residence, Gorki chose Capri for its mild climate and beautiful scenery. For seven years his Villa Serafina became a place of pilgrimage for people from

all over the world, especially for Russian revolutionaries, who were in need of hope, strength, and advice,
which they expected and received from Gorki.

The trip to America had refurbished the writer's
optimism: "Each day convinces me more that the world
revolution is close at hand." His undoubting faith in the
victory of the revolution finds special expression in the
play that he wrote in America, *The Enemies,* and in his
famous novel *The Mother.* In both works he portrayed
the unknown strength residing in the masses. The drama
The Enemies uncovers the hypocrisy of the liberals,who
are ready to sell their country, the people, honor, and
freedom to save their own skins. *The Mother* was first
published in English in the United States and in London
in 1906. Before its publication in book form, the novel
had appeared in installments published between July 2
and October 30, 1907, in the feuilleton section of
Vorwärts in Berlin. In Russia, only the first part was
printed in Volume XVI of *Snaniye;* it was censored beyond recognition. The publication resulted immediately in a warrant issued by the St. Petersburg city commander for the "member of the painters' guild, master
A. M. Peshkov."

The models for the characters of Pavel Vlasov and
his mother Nilovna in *The Mother* were the revolutionary worker Pyotr Salomov, who had been condemned
by the czarist courts for participation in the demonstrations of May 1902 in Sormovo, and his mother, who,
disguised as a pilgrim, had spread revolutionary writings through the whole country. Gorki had also known
a mother who had been tried in Ufa because she had
smuggled bombs into prison to her son. The novel was
a monument for them and for many other heroic moth-
ers Gorki had known. For the first time in Russian
literature he described the change from the spontaneous,

unorganized struggles of the working class to organized
action. He described this change with so much personal
involvement and such a sense of realism that these characters became not creations of fantasy but people of
flesh and blood. Lenin called this work of contemporary
history "a very timely book." The wife of Karl Kautsky
wrote to Gorki's companion M. F. Andreyeva:

This wonderful novel belongs among the most beautiful pieces that
Gorki has ever written. It radiates a sincere, noble warmth and pene-
trates immediately to the heart; it kindles a fire that glows for a long
time. One feels that the author has written this novel with his heart's
blood, so complete is his identification with his characters. How one
must love his mother, how one suffers with her, how one appreciates
her more from page to page! Please tell your Aleksei how most sincerely I want to thank him for this book.

The book was translated into all major languages
and became a world success. As was to be expected, the
reviews of the bourgeois and reactionary critics were
negative; in this they followed the Russian author D.
W. Filosofov, who had initiated a campaign against the
author in his essay "Gorki's End."

In the spring of 1907, the fifth congress of the
Russian Social Democratic Party met in London.
Gorki listened by the hour in Whitechapel Church to
the impassioned debates between the Mensheviks led by
Plekhanov and the Bolsheviks led by Lenin. In his *Reminiscences of Lenin* he recorded the impressions that
the great politician made on him at that time:

I found out for the first time in my life that the most complicated questions of politics can be dealt with in the simplest manner. This man did
not attempt to turn out pretty phrases; he handed out each word as on
a platter and uncovered its meaning in the most surprisingly exact
manner.

At midnight on July 1, when the congress adjourned
after the thirty-fifth session, all the Bolsheviks' resolu-
tions had been passed.

From those days dates the friendship between Gorki and Lenin: "His relationship to me was that of a strict teacher and of a good, concerned friend," Gorki wrote. Lenin often visited Capri, constantly worried about the health of the tubercular writer, and was interested in the progress of his work. He recognized in Gorki a powerful ally in a common cause:

Gorki is undoubtedly an artist of major importance; he has been and will continue to be extremely useful for the proletarian movement in the world.

In the fall of 1908, arguments broke out within the Social Democratic Party when Gorki, Lunacharski, Bogdanov, and others deviated from Plekhanov's strictly materialistic philosophy. In the periodical *The Proletarian* and in his book *Materialism and Empiriocriticism* Lenin turned against this renegade group of "God-seekers." At the same time and with the active support of Gorki, a school was instituted on the lower floor of the Villa Serafina to train Russian workers for propaganda purposes. Lenin interpreted this as an attempt to build up an organization of Bogdanov's followers and therefore refused to lecture to this group. In *The Proletarian* of July 1909, he issued a strong statement against the attempt of a few comrades "to combine social democracy with the preaching of faith and religion and to endow scientific socialism with the character of a religious faith." Lenin called these efforts "a form of opposition by petty bourgeois tendencies against proletarian socialism, that is, Marxism," and the initiators of this school were branded as representatives of "Otsovism" and the "creation of God." Bogdanov and his followers, among them Gorki, then published the paper *Ahead* to represent their own group. The disagreement led to rumors that Gorki had been excluded from the Social Democratic Party.

Gorki gave lectures in the school in Capri on the history of Russian literature and contributed research on Pushkin and Tolstoi. His thoughts were further expressed in a series of excellent essays, notably "The Disintegration of Personality," in which Gorki refutes the myth that only the ruling class is capable of creative achievements and that only the individual, living withdrawn and secluded, is in a position to create works of art:

The people not only constitute the source that alone creates all material values; they also form the only inexhaustible fount of spiritual values. They are the primeval sages and poets, who have created all the great poetry as well as all the tragedies of the world, and among these works the greatest of all—the history of the culture of the entire world.

At the height of the disagreement between Lenin and the Bogdanov group, Gorki wrote the story "A Confession," published in 1908 by Snaniye. It portrays the inner struggle of a man who would like to fuse Christianity and Marxism. The novella *A Summer,* written in 1909, deals with the role of the farmer in the revolution.

After the discord between Gorki and Lenin had been settled in 1910, Gorki gave a few of his *Russian Fairy Tales* to *Svesda,* the new journal of the Bolsheviks. Lenin called these tales "revolutionary proclamations." Outside the party press, Gorki wrote on events of the public and literary life and above all worked on new plans. He kept his old habit of observing his surroundings very minutely even while at Capri. As a result, several narrations on the simple everyday life of lower-class people were written under the collective title *Italian Tales,* although they contain nothing fantastic or improbable and are in no way typically Italian. Whatever his milieu, Gorki remained above all a great Russian writer.

During his exile he wrote his masterly descriptions of the Russian provinces, which he had studied in detail and come to hate, especially during his exile to Arsamas. In the pieces written between 1909 and 1911, in the story "The Little Town of Okurov," in the novel *The Life of Matvey Koshemyakin,* in the plays *The Odd Men* and *Vasa Shelesnova,* he portrayed the indecisive, backward, and reactionary world of the petty bourgeois of 1905.

On the occasion of the three-hundredth anniversary of the house of Romanov, the czar granted amnesty and Gorki, terribly homesick, planned to return to Russia. His departure was delayed, however, by a serious tubercular relapse. Lenin wrote to express his concern: "I am terribly afraid that the return in winter may damage your health." Gorki recovered, however, and toward the end of December 1913 he was ready to leave. He settled in Finland, close to St. Petersburg.

6

Fighting for Peace and Justice

Late in 1913, *My Childhood*, the first volume of Gorki's autobiographical trilogy, was published. Ever since his first literary success in Nishni, he had wanted to write this autobiography. In the first volume he not only records the thoughts, early observations, and experiences of the child, but provides a valuable document of the political and cultural history of czarist Russia, recounting the sufferings, the wisdom, and the strength of the Russian people. In *Through Russia*, another work published at this time, Gorki produced a collection of stories and sketches about people that he had met on his journeys, skillfully and lovingly describing the customs and songs of little-known tribes.

During his sojourn at Capri, Gorki had reread all of Dostoevski's work and had become increasingly convinced that the entire decadent movement had originated with that author. In 1913, when the Art Theater wished to perform a dramatization of *The Possessed*, Gorki wrote the severe attack "On Karamazovism":

Beyond question or doubt Dostoevski is a genius, but an evil genius. He felt and understood with extraordinarily profound insight and he elaborated with great joy the two sicknessess that a dreadful history and a laborious, sinful life have cultivated in the Russian people: the sadistic cruelty of the nihilist who has been cheated out of everything and, at the opposite extreme, the masochism of the humiliated and fearful creature who goes so far as to enjoy his own suffering, while at the same time parading it, not without evil satisfaction, in front of all the world and himself. This kind of man is mercilessly downtrodden and is proud of it. Why does one want to draw the attention of society to these sick phenomena of our national psyche, to its deformities? To overcome them and to heal them should constitute our most urgent task. It is necessary to create a healthy atmosphere in which we have no room for these sicknesses.

The Possessed was performed despite this protest, and the reactionary papers once again had good reason to attack Gorki violently. His drama *The Old Man*

(1915) is explicitly directed against Dostoevski.

Many of the writers who had participated in the Snaniye project gradually became reactionaries, with the result that in 1912 Gorki, severely disappointed, withdrew from the publishing house and decided to involve himself even more closely than before with the proletarian writers. He never forgot how difficult his own road to success had been—how only hard and un-interrupted work had brought him mastery. He passed his experiences on to young authors who had come to him for help and he was extremely magnanimous. He repeatedly reminded the young people to be simple and true: "Don't be influenced by the fashionable writers or the artificers of words. Truth and simplicity are two sisters and beauty is the third." Most of these aspiring authors came from the common people. With great care Gorki advised his young colleagues, attempted to im-prove their manuscripts, paid attention to the most minute details, and noted the smallest mistakes. He never forgot to point out that writers who wished to ded-icate their lives to their work must never remove them-selves from the people. In this regard he advised the working-class author Travin:

Don't concentrate exclusively on yourself and don't write about just your life and your thoughts; think of the hundreds of thousands of people in situations similar to or even more difficult than yours. Try to find the thoughts, emotions, and aspirations common to all work-ers and explain them briefly, strongly, and simply.

He also warned against seclusion:

Most contemporary writers live as on an uninhabited island, outside of life. . . . One should not be a Robinson Crusoe ever! One has to live, to scream, to laugh, to complain, to love. . . . A writer should be the echo of the world and not the nursemaid of his own soul.

He repeatedly stressed the importance of the living language as the one material with which an author has to work. He advised young writers to study this language, to enlarge their vocabulary, and to rejoice over each new word:

for language lives a complex life, changes, has a destiny of its own, and this destiny mirrors the history of the people. . . . It is good for the writer to battle with the word, but the battle should be joyful.

To further the new realistic movement, whose rebirth he had predicted in an essay in *Pravda* on January 26, 1914, he edited the first *Anthology of Proletarian Writers* and wrote in the introduction: "One day, this volume will be considered one of the first steps of the Russian proletariat toward the creation of its own literature."

The outbreak of World War I deeply upset Gorki, and from its inception he was one of its most violent opponents. He even broke with his adopted son Sinovi, who started his military career as a volunteer in a regiment of the French Foreign Legion especially reserved for Russians. (Sinovi is now a French general and retired attaché in Paris. He has been awarded the highest French honors: the Great Cross of the Legion D'Honneur, the Cross of War, and the Military Medaille.)

In meetings and essays Gorki spoke passionately for pacifism and turned against every kind of oppression. On December 8, 1915, the first edition of *Lepotis* was published, with Gorki as general editor. *Lepotis* was the only Russian journal that fought nationalism and imperialism and called for peace in a Europe united and without national boundaries. The first edition of 10,000 copies sold out immediately. In this periodical Gorki attempted to reach such internationally known socialists and pacifists as George Bernard Shaw, Romain Rolland, and H. G. Wells, "who stand outside the chaos of passion, stirred up through a mad war and destroying millions of the most active and creative people of our planet." In addition, the journal was intended as a means of introducing young authors to the public. It contained the first printing of Mayakovski's poem "War and Peace," in which the poet attempted, as he said, "to spit with verses into the face of war."

Lepotis and the publishing house Parus distributed their brochures in all major cities and even villages, swiftly attracting the animosity of all reactionary and pro-war circles. These groups later venomously remarked that "Maksim the Great is today not only the king of rogues, but also a tremendous publisher," and they asked for incisive measures on the part of the authorities. The police immediately obliged and in a report specifically stressed the "Social Democratic tendencies and the defeatism" of the paper. After the assassination of Rasputin, however, they did not have time to close the firm. *Lepotis* existed for another year, suspending publication because of difficulties with the printers.

When the czarist government held the Jews responsible for the defeats on the Western front and persecuted them, Gorki fervently defended them. He edited the collection *The Shield,* to which all the great writers of Russia contributed. The profits from the sale were to benefit the Jewish refugees.

In 1916, Gorki published the second volume of his autobiography, *In the World,* dealing with the hard years of apprenticeship that led him to understand that "the life we lead is not worth anything. We have to provide a better life."

In December 1916, he decided to edit a series of books for young people. The best writers from all over the world were to contribute to this series. Wishing to

publish the biographies of great men, he wrote to
Romain Rolland:

In these dire times, nobody needs good care as much as the children.
. . . Let us remind them that among all nations great men and noble
hearts have existed and still do to this day. This senseless war is the
most blatant proof of our moral weakness, of the decline of our culture.
Let us remind the children that men have not always been as weak
and evil as they are—unfortunately—now.

Rolland was to write on Beethoven, Wells on Edison,
Nansen on Columbus, and Gorki on Garibaldi. His
letter to Wells contains these beautiful lines:

Now perhaps more than at any other time our children are the most
precious and most essential hope for this earth. . . . One must purify
the children's hearts from the bloody rust of this senseless and terrible
war; one must replant in the hearts of our youth a faith in and veneration for mankind.

Early in 1917, food supplies in Russia became so
scarce that strikes and demonstrations started in St.
Petersburg. In February the workers and the military
joined. On March 2 the czar abdicated, a provisional
government took over, and soon the bourgeois-demo-
cratic revolution swept through the whole country.

In the newly published newspaper *Novaya Shisn,*
Gorki passionately celebrated the liberation from the
czar, while opposing the imperialistic plans of the
Milyukov and Kerenski governments which were not
inclined to satisfy the people's demand for peace. The
war continued. After witnessing the course of domestic
events, Gorki sided with the Bolsheviks, whom Kerenski attempted to eliminate. Gorki's articles were usually
printed on the front page of the paper and under the
title "Untimely Thoughts." He still hoped for a pact
between the workers and the intelligentsia.

In the summer of 1917, Russia came close to civil
war. The Bolsheviks became increasingly dominant in

the workers' and soldiers' councils. Gorki was horrified at Lenin's thesis on "the end of the peaceful revolution" and the announcement of violent conflict. Believing that this could lead only "to anarchy and the decline of the proletariat and the revolution," he courageously spoke against all "bloody combat."

On October 24, 1917, the October Revolution began, under the leadership of Lenin. The major fighting occurred on October 25 (November 17, according to the new calendar). The provisional government was overthrown and the Russian Socialist Federated Soviet Republic was proclaimed. The next day, the second All-Russian Congress of the Soviets adopted the historical decrees "On Peace" and "On Land." Gorki, full of distrust and disapproval, watched the bloody fights, the demolitions, and the arrest of old revolutionaries— all "horrifying undertakings, as committed by Plehve and Stolypin." He was not afraid of attacking Lenin and Trotski publicly. He wrote about the "degeneration of socialism" until *Pravda* accused him of speaking "the language of the enemies of the working class." Not surprisingly the Bolsheviks frequently censored Gorki's newspaper and fined him heavily for printing unfavorable news. *Novaya Shisn* then appeared, as in the old regime, though under a different name.

On the other hand, Gorki supported Lenin's endeavors to end the war:

... since three years of cruel, senseless slaughter have passed, since for three years the blood of the best nations in the world has been wasted and the most valuable brains of Europe have been destroyed. ... No justification exists for this abominable self-destruction. In this twentieth century, humanism is forgotten and ridiculed; all that has been created by the selfless dedication of science has been usurped by murderers and is now used to destroy mankind. Whatever these hypocrites may say about the grandiose goal of war, their lies cannot conceal the outrageous and shameful truth: this war was born out of

avarice, the only goddess that the *"realpolitiker"*—these murderers
who do business with the life of the people—recognize and admire.

Gorki likewise agreed with Lenin on his assessment of
the politics of the Entente toward the Soviet Union.

The socialist and idealist Maksim Gorki could not
be confined to the narrow limits of a party program. He
declared that he had "an organic aversion to politics."
In his own way, however, he attempted to help and alleviate the sufferings of his beloved Russian people. He was
indefatigable in his attempts to protect cultural monu-
ments during the time of the revolution. He founded
the Committee for the Preservation of Works of Art and
organized a society for the education of the people, called
"Freedom and Culture." Remembering the spiritual
starvation that had marred his youth, he attempted to
make science and the arts accessible to all strata of society, as in his establishment of the publishing house
World Literature (1919), which was to make available
the best works of classical writers from all over the
world. In 1918, he supported the foundation of the first
workers' and farmers' university in Petrograd, edited the
children's newspaper *Aurora Borealis,* and in 1920, es-
tablished the Commission to Fight Juvenile Delinquen-
cy. *Yeralesh,* a collection of stories for children, and a
second *Anthology of Proletarian Writers* were published
in 1918. To provide contemporary authors and critics
with "a piece of bread and a little warmth," Gorki made
the "House of Arts" available to them.

It is impossible to enumerate all the organizations in
which he participated. He took all these activities very
seriously: "New men are created by new conditions of
existence—and new conditions create new men." He
led discussions, made telephone calls, wrote to the authorities, to the government, and when nothing else

succeeded, even to Lenin himself, until he was totally exhausted. "I am sorry I have to bother you again," he wrote almost every day, "I have no other way." When letters were not successful, he subjected himself to a twenty-hour train ride to Moscow, to speak personally with Lenin. He saved the lives of many through his imploring petitions. He often spoke with Lenin about the cruelties of the revolutionary tactics. "What do you want?" Lenin asked him, amazed and angry:

How can humanity be possible in a revolution of such unprecedented magnitude? Where can you find the opportunity to be soft-hearted and generous? Don't you think you are dallying in nonsense and pettiness? You compromise yourself in the eyes of your comrades!

Gorki did not become discouraged, however, because he believed that "senseless cruelty too, compromises you and damages your cause by alienating much potential help, thereby excluding it from cooperating with you." Despite Lenin's skeptical attitude toward the intelligentsia—who, as he thought, had betrayed the workers on many accounts—and despite his heated words with Gorki, he never refused any of Gorki's requests.

Whenever Gorki read to the soldiers of the Red Army—to workers, students, and women—the crowds turned out in vast numbers, because the revolutionaries were eager for literature. In 1919, Gorki published his recollections of Tolstoi and Andreyev and, in the newspaper *Communist International,* he wrote articles against the intervention of the Entente and the white-guard counterrevolution. During the terrible famine of 1919–1920, Gorki was made chairman of the Central Committee for the Improvement of the Living Conditions of Scientists, and on Lenin's suggestion he appealed to the West to help the starving Russian population.

Considering his turbulent life and his constant worries about others, it is not surprising that Gorki's tuberculosis worsened. Lenin, seriously concerned, but at the same time hoping to rid himself of an inconvenient presence, persuaded Gorki to take a cure abroad. "You cough up blood, but you don't leave. Please don't be stubborn, I implore you, take the trip and cure yourself." Finally, in October of 1921, Gorki followed Lenin's advice and went to the Black Forest and to Switzerland. After spending the subsequent summer on the Baltic Sea at Spa Heringsdorf, he rented, in fall of 1922, a former rest home in Bad Saarow near Berlin on the Scharmützel Lake. He lived there with his son Maksim, his daughter-in-law Timosha, and a few friends. He finished the third part of his autobiography, *My University Days,* as well as the *Reminiscences of Korolenko,* and with a small group of young authors he founded the literary-scientific paper *Beseda,* which was to acquaint the Russian reader with such modern Western authors as Stefan Zweig, H. G. Wells, Romain Rolland, Henri Barbusse, George Bernard Shaw, and John Galsworthy.

When the news of Lenin's death reached him in January of 1924, Gorki was profoundly shaken: "Not even for Tolstoi did I mourn in this manner. My heart grows heavy. The helmsman has left the ship. . . ." He sent a wreath with the simple dedication "Farewell, my friend" and immediately began to write the *Reminiscences of V. I. Lenin,* which was to be published immediately in the United States, France, and Russia. He rewrote these memoirs several times, the last time in 1931. The portrait belongs among the most splendid presentations of the founder of the Soviet Union:

He was simple and honest, like everything he said. His heroism lacked all external splendor. It consisted in the humble, ascetic, self-sacrificing activities of an honest Russian intellectual and revolutionary who was firmly convinced of the possibility of social justice on this earth. His heroism renounced all the joys of the world to dedicate itself completely to the happiness of mankind.

After a short stay in Freiburg and Marienbad, the Italian government granted Gorki, in March of 1924, the permission to settle in Sorrento. He rented the villa Il Sorrito, situated in a lovely lemon and olive grove, stretching to the sea. A number of important works were to be written there over the next four years. In 1925 he completed the novel *The Artamonovs,* dedicated to Romain Rolland. The story of a degenerating family of merchants, pursued over three generations, had occupied him since his first encounter with Tolstoi in 1902. He had even discussed it with Lenin in 1910. Lenin had listened with great attention and then had said, "A magnificent topic, but I don't see how you could carry it to its conclusion. Reality does not offer a conclusion. No, it must be written after the revolution." Gorki was finally able to carry his story to a historically consequential ending, portraying the decline of the bourgeoisie as the end of a "system of society that was inimical to mankind."

He then began the multivolume novel *The Life of Klim Samgin:* "This will be a voluminous undertaking. Less of a novel, I think, and more of a chronicle from the 1880's to 1918. I will have to work on it for a long time, a year and longer. . . ." In this work he mercilessly uncovers, by means of "imaginary people," the part of the Russian intelligentsia that played a false game and that was constantly prepared to betray the interests of the people and of the revolution. The Soviet Encyclopedia calls this work "the most expansive and mature, characterized by the unusual wealth of realism, profound exposure to the most salient contradictions of reality, breadth of epic representation, and much philosophical thought." It is the final account of Gorki's observations of Russian life within the span of forty years. The work was never completed. Only three volumes had been published when Gorki died.

While working on this novel, Gorki continued to write his *Reminiscences of Contemporaries,* especially those of Krassin and Yesenin, as well as articles and several stories, notably "Anecdote," which provided the material for his play *Yegor Bulychev.*

He followed the events in Russia with great interest. Although he frequently criticized the regime, he also defended it vociferously against attacks from foreign countries. Best known of all are his polemics against the White Russian emigrés and against the trial and execution in the United States of the alleged anarchists Sacco and Vanzetti. He repeatedly rose to speak for peace, democracy, and socialism.

Gorki read his mail, which he received from all over the world, with great patience and attentiveness. Petitions, thank-you notes, letters from friends, and above all manuscripts that he was asked to evaluate arrived steadily. In Sorrento, as on Capri and in Moscow, he remained the counselor, teacher, and friend of the new generation of authors. In 1928, he described his experiences in the essay "How I Learned to Write." Virtually every significant writer of the time found stimulation and encouragement in Gorki: Mayakovski, Sholokhov, Ostrovski, Leonov, Gladkov, Makarenko, Pavlenko, Fedin, Aleksei Tolstoi, and many more.

7

Last
Years

Gorki returned to Russia on May 28, 1928. He was received with great honors, and his sixtieth birthday was celebrated all over the country. His dream of revisiting the sites of his childhood and youth became a reality. He drove along the streets through which he had wandered long ago. He was overcome by the wealth of new impressions, later recording them in *Across the Soviet Union*: "What surprised me most was the active, challenging attitude to life that has grown tremendously in these years."

The subsequent years were filled with creative activities. He was the leader of the literary life in the Soviet Union. He founded and edited a number of newspapers and participated in several significant literary ventures. At his initiative, several large collections were published, including *The History of a Young Man of the Nineteenth Century, One Day in Our World, History of the Civil War, History of Factories and Plants,* and *The Library of Novels.* He also took care of his enormous correspondence, studied the living conditions of abandoned children in reformatories, and still found strength and time for his own creative writing. Until 1932, the government gave him permission to pass the winter months in Sorrento, because of his ill health.

Between 1931 and 1933, he wrote the plays *Yegor Bulychev and the Others, Somov and the Others,* and *Dostigeyev and the Others,* which he planned as a dramatic cycle representing the decline of the bourgeoisie and the victory of socialism.

In 1932, the Soviet Union celebrated the fortieth anniversary of Gorki's literary career. Stalin decorated him with the Order of Lenin and wrote to him: "With all my heart I wish you many more creative years, to the enjoyment of all workers and to the horror of all enemies of the working class." Gorki's birthplace, Nishni-Nov-

gorod, was renamed "Gorki" and many schools, the-
aters—even the Moscow Art Theater—the Institute for
World Literature in the Academy of Sciences, and a
main street in Moscow came to bear his name.

The topics of his essays during these years were
primarily decided by the consequences of the economic
crisis: the growth of fascism and anti-Semitism and the
related anti-Soviet campaigns. Gorki's endeavors were
directed toward maintaining world peace. He spoke
against the increase of racism all over the world and
wrote in his essay "On Inhumanity":

Throughout my life I was a pacifist. The war made me ill and ashamed
for mankind, and full of hatred against the planners of mass murder
and the destroyers of life. . . .

Gorki strongly condemned the new dictatorship of
Hitler's Nazism, and on February 4, 1933, Germany
confiscated all of Gorki's writings that had so far appeared in German translation. On May 6, 1933, Gorki
wrote to Romain Rolland:

In the country of Goethe, Humboldt, Helmholtz, and a great number
of enormously talented and gifted men, the wonderful masters and
founders of culture—in this country, a boastful adventurer, a little man
with little understanding, an untalented imitator of the skilled actor
Mussolini, barbaric and without any sense of responsibility, holds
command. In this country, they now advertize renunciation of culture,
regression not only to the Middle Ages but to the times of the Nibe-
lungen. Someone already screams: "Down with Christ, long live
Wotan" . . . and again the persecution of the Jews!

In May 1934, Gorki suffered a great loss when his
only son Maksim died. His impetus to work remained
unimpaired, however, even though he lived "full of evil
thoughts and not at peace with the world." Gorki hid his
sorrow and sadness in ceaseless activity, but in no way
closed his eyes to Stalin's increasing terror. As under
Lenin, he protested the measures taken by the dictator's

secret police and through his petitions saved the lives of friends and enemies.

After opening the First Congress of Soviet Authors in August 1934, he was elected chairman. On this occasion he gave a long speech on the artistic methods of socialist realism and its further development.

On March 22, 1936, he wrote to Rolland from Teseli in the Crimea, where he had been staying for a few months:

The almond trees are already in blossom and the spring hurries to impress us once again with its display of energy. I work a great deal, complete nothing, grow awfully tired.... I am afraid of only one thing: that the heart might stop before I can finish the novel [*Klim Samgin*].

Early in May, he was back in Moscow.

He fell ill with influenza and his health worsened every day. On June 18, 1936, Radio Moscow announced his death. During the spectacular burial ceremonies, his urn was deposited on a high pedestal in front of the Lenin mausoleum and Molotov gave a memorable speech:

In this moment we all feel as though a bright segment of our lives has left us forever.... The workers and everyone working see themselves reflected in Gorki. They see their own lives, their own destiny, their own future. For this reason, all workers in our country and in other countries as well loved Gorki so deeply. They still love him and always will.... His greatness consists in the fact that his bright mind, his closeness to the people, his gigantic, selfless struggles for cultural values to benefit mankind, have made him the boundless friend of all the working people.

Khrushchev and Bulganin were in the honor guard. Stalin, Molotov, Ordshonikidse, and Kaganovich finally carried the urn to the Kremlin wall, where it was immured. A simple commemorative plate states only the name, and the dates of birth and death.

Three interpretations of Gorki's death exist. When, in 1938, the Bukharin show trial took place, Yagoda, the accused chief of the secret police, confessed to murdering Gorki's son Maksim and then the writer himself. He said that he had done this under the order of the Trotskyites and with the help of the equally accused Professor Pletnyov and the Kremlin physician Dr. Levin. Within twenty-four hours, Gorki was given "forty camphor injections . . . as well as two Digalen, four caffein, and two strychnine injections." The second version states that Stalin himself wished to stifle Gorki's constant criticism by having the writer murdered. Yagoda had acted under Stalin's orders and was then accused of the crime so that he could be eliminated as a witness.

New information on the subject has been found in Moscow's Gorki Museum, which houses the central archives for Gorki research, comprising much material on the life and work of the writer. This information indicates that an autopsy of the corpse had revealed the full extent of the tubercular devastation; at the time of death, only one-third of the lung tissues had not yet been attacked. According to this report Gorki was simply unable to recover from the serious influenza on which the Moscow newspapers had commented every day during his illness.

Gorki's humanistic realism is a new creative endeavor and its effects far transcend the borders of Russian literature. Gorki not only opened a new field for world literature by enriching it with new material, but he also created a new and exemplary form and method. Maksim Gorki's Russian people stood up to defend the oppressed and outcast not only of czarist Russia, but of the entire world.

Lion Feuchtwanger

Chronology

1861: Abolition of serfdom in Russia.

1868: Maksim Gorki born on March 16 in Nishni-Novgorod.

1870: Aleksander Herzen dies.

1872: The first volume of Karl Marx's *Das Kapital* forbidden in Russia.

1874: Universal military service in Russia.

1876–1878: Gorki goes to school.

1878–1884: Years of apprenticeship.

1878: Russian peace treaty with Turkey. German legislation concerning the socialists.

1881: Attempted assassination of Czar Aleksander II. Dostoevski dies.

1883: Karl Marx dies in London. Turgenev dies.

1884: Gorki moves to Kazan.

1884–1887: Works as cargo hauler, servant, baker, livery boy.

1887: Lenin at the University of Kazan. Lenin's brother Aleksander is executed as a revolutionary. The so-called "legislation for cooks" bars education for children of workers and the lower classes.

1887:   Gorki attempts suicide.

1888–1889:   First and second journeys across Russia.

1889 (fall):   Arrested in Nishni. Visit with Korolenko.

1889:   Founding of the Second International in Paris.

1890–1891:   Two-year journey across Russia. Spends fall in Tiflis.

1891–1892:   Famine in Russia.

1892:   Moves to Nishni. Friendship with Korolenko. "Makar Chudra," Gorki's first story.

1892:   Increase of strike movements in Russia.

1893:   Franco-Russian pact. *Yemalyan Pilyay* (novella). Death of the composer Tchaikovsky.

1894:   Nicholas II becomes czar.

1895:   Gorki becomes editor of the *Samarskaya Gazeta.* "Chelkash"; "The Song of the Falcon"; "Old Isergil."

1896:   Marries the proofreader Y. P. Volshina. Moves to Nishni. Works as an editor. Contracts tuberculosis.

1897:   "Orloff and His Wife"; "Malva"; "Country Fair at Goldva"; "The Good-for-Nothing."

1898:   Arrested in Nishni.

1899:   Contributes to many newspapers. *Foma Gordeyev* (first novel).

1900:   Meets Tolstoi. Until 1912 member of the Snaniye publishing house. *Three of Them* (second novel).

1901:   Arrest in Nishni (April–May).

1901–1902:   Sojourn in the Crimea, then in St. Petersburg. "The Song of the Firebird."

1902:   Performance of *The Petty Bourgeois* (March) and *The Lower Depths* (December).

1904:   Performance of *Summer Guests* (November).

1904:   Chekhov dies.

1904–1905:   Russo-Japanese War.

1905:   Gorki arrested in St. Petersburg. Sojourn in Finland.

Works for *Novaya Shisn* (under Lenin). *Children of the Sun; The Barbarians; Remarks Concerning the Petty Bourgeoisie.*

1906: Travels to the United States via Germany, Switzerland, and France. Settles in Capri. *The Enemies.* American sketches and pamphlets. *The Mother.*

1907: Trip to London. Beginning of friendship with Lenin.

1908: *The Disintegration of Personality; A Confession.*

1910: Lev Tolstoi dies.

1910: *Vassa Shelesnova; The Strangers.*

1912: Independent Bolshevist section in the czarist duma.

1913: Returns to Russia. *My Childhood.*

1914: Beginning of World War I.

1915–1916: Editor-in-chief of *Lepotis. In the World.*

1917: The Great October Revolution.

1917–1921: Contributes to various societies and organizations. Founding of the publishing house World Literature. Renewed attack of tuberculosis.

1918: Peace treaty of Brest-Litovsk. Attempted assassination of Lenin.

1919: Founding of the Communist International.

1922: Mussolini seizes power.

1923: *My University Days.*

1924: Lenin dies. Gorki settles in Sorrento.

1925: *The Artamonovs.*

1927–1930: *The Life of Klim Samgin* (first volume, 1927; second volume, 1928; third volume,1930; fourth volume published posthumously from his notes).

1928: First five-year plan in the Soviet Union. Gorki returns to Russia.

1929: World economic crisis.

1931: *Somov and the Others* (drama).

1932: Last trip to Italy. *Yegor Bulychev and the Others; On Whose Side Are You, Cultural Leaders?*

1933:   Second five-year plan. Hitler seizes power in Germany.
        Dostigeyev and the Others; On Education through Truth.
1934:   *On Soviet Literature; On Language; Proletarian Literature.*
1935:   Soviet Union becomes member of the League of Nations.
1936:   Gorki dies in Moscow on June 18.

Selected Bibliography

Works by Maksim Gorki

Chelkash, 1895, story (*Tchelkache*, 1902)

Malva, 1897, story (*Malva*, 1901)

Konovalov, 1897, story (*Konovalov*, 1901)

Byvshiye lyudi, 1897, story (*Creatures That Once Were Men*, 1901)

Suprugi Orlovy, 1897, story (*Orloff and His Wife*, 1901)

Dvadtzat shest i odna, 1899, story (*Twenty-six Men and a Girl*, 1902)

Foma Gordeyev, 1899, novel (*Foma Gordeyev*, 1901)

Meshchane, 1901, play (*The Smug Citizen*, 1906)

Troye, 1901, novel (*Three of Them*, 1902)

A. P. Chekhov, 1905 (*Chekhov*, 1905)

Mat, 1906, novel (*The Mother*, 1906)

Shisn nenushnovo cheloveka, 1907, story (*The Spy: The Story of a Superfluous Man*, 1908)

Ispoved, 1908, story (*A Confession*, 1909)

Gorodok Okurov, 1909, story

Shisn Matveya Koshemyakina, 1910, novel (*The Life of*

Matvei Kozhemyakin, 1959)

Detstvo, 1912–13 (*My Childhood,* 1915; also in *Autobiography,* 1939)

Vlyudyakh, 1914 (*In the World,* 1917; also in *Autobiography,* 1939)

Po Rusi, 1915, stories and sketches (*Through Russia,* 1921)

Vozpominaniya o Lev Nikolayeviche Tolstoi, 1919 (*Reminiscences of Lev Nikolaevich Tolstoy,* 1920)

L. Andreyev, 1922 (*Andreev,* 1922)

Moi universitety, 1922 (*My University Days;* also *My Universities,* 1923; also in *Autobiography,* 1939)

Delo Artamonovykh, 1925, novel (*Decadence,* 1927; new translation, *The Artamonovs,* 1957)

Shisn Klima Samgina, 1927–32, novel (*The Life of Klim Samgin:* I., *The Bystander* 1930; II., *The Magnet,* 1931; III., *Other Fires,* 1933; IV., *The Spectre,* 1938)

Sobraniye sochinenii, 1949–56, collected works

Works about Maksim Gorki

Barras, F. M. *Maxim Gorky, the Writer: An Interpretation.* 1967

Chukovski, K. *Gorkovskiye chteniya.* 1947 ff.

Hare, Richard. *Maxim Gorky, Romantic Realist and Conservative Revolutionary.* 1962

Kaun, A. *Maxim Gorky and His Russia.* 1932

Khodasevish, V. *Nekropol, "Gorkii."* 1939

Weil, Irwin. *Gorky.* 1966

Wolfe, Bertram D. *Bridge and the Abyss: The Troubled Friendship of Maxim Gorky and V. I. Lenin,* 1967.

Index